One Way Conversations

Copyright © 2018 Owen Ness

All rights reserved.

ISBN:
ISBN - 9781721763566

Forward:

Many people, over the years have suggested that I should write my memoirs. I have chosen to call it 'One Way Conversations'. This is intended as a background for what you will read in the following pages.

This collection covers various events over the years starting with my early life on the farm. I went to Howick high school.

This was followed by grade 12 matric. at Westmount High because I needed grade 12 to go to Royal Military College and become a pilot.

After the year at Westmount I lost interest in being a pilot and my father registered me at MacDonald College. I qualified to enter second year.

After graduating with a bachelor's degree Dr. Crampton, who was head of the nutrition department, and my uncle Professor Alex Ness talked me into taking post-graduate studies.

After two years without completing my degree I took a position with Alcan dealing with the problems of fluoride pollution and it's effects on dairy cattle.

After six years I had an opportunity to apply to the Centre D'Étude Industrielle in Geneva, Switzerland. This advanced business management school was created by Alcan to prepare managers to make Alcan the most international company in the world.

When I returned from Geneva I returned to my previous job dealing with pollution.

In 1996 I was transferred to personnel management at Arvida Works, this was a complete career change.

In 1971 because my oldest son David and second oldest Peter had to have kidney transplants requiring a move to Montreal into what became an international responsibility. In 1979 I was transferred to Britain.

In 1985 I returned to Montreal. I was an administrative manager of the laboratories. This position lasted for less than a year when I returned to personnel with the responsibility for the North and South America.

In 1988 I went into my final job as Vice President – Personnel - the top personnel position in Alcan.

I retired in 1993.

As most of you know I have rather crooked fingers caused by rheumatoid arthritis. Without the help of Brenda Elder and Beverly Hynes who are amongst my caregivers I would not have been able to carry out this project.

Finally I want to thank my partner, Annette Mariotti, for encouraging me to complete these conversations.

TABLE OF CONTENTS

MY EARLY YEARS 6

MY FIRST DAY ON THE JOB 15

MY SEVENTEEN YEARS IN THE SAGUENAY 23

THE MOST IMPORTANT YEAR OF MY LIFE 37

ADRIAN PLOURDE 46

THE HUMAN SIDE OF ENTERPRISE 57

MY ROLL OF HONOUR 64

FRIENDS, TEACHERS BOSSES & EMPLOYEES 78

NOBODY PROMISED A BED OF ROSES 85

MORE ABOUT THE FAMILY 96

ARLIE 105

FIVE YEARS IN BRITAIN 113

A SHORT CAREER BACK IN RESEARCH 139

THE FINAL CHAPTER 145

A TRIBUTE TO ARLIE 150

THE TWO MISSING CHAPTERS 153

MY EARLY YEARS

Owen MacGregor Ness was born on the family farm on the third day of April 1930. Probably not a great gift to my parents right at the heart of the depression. They never showed any resentment and were always wonderful to me.

Naturally, I don't have much memory of the early years, but I do remember three events when I was five years old. I still have the scar on my left index finger from showing my sister how to cut up sugar beets to avoid the cows choking on them. I have no idea who left the knife where I could get it. I remember the school bus driving by as we headed off to the doctor's office in Ormstown.

The second incident was not a conscious attempt to return to the doctor's office. My father was talking to the Postmaster and store keeper in the village store and my life-long curiosity took me to the back of the store which was quite dark. I walked over an entrance to the basement which should have been covered by a trap door. I remembered afterwards seeing a big police dog straining on his chain as he advised my father and Mr. Gebbie that something was wrong. I still have the scar under my lower lip and it is alleged that I bit off the end of my tongue. I don't actually believe that because I can't figure out how my lower teeth could go through my lower lip and bite off my tongue at the same time.

The third incident is more fixed in time. There had been a big storm during the night which blew off the large barn door and turned the hay loader upside down where it had been left in the hayfield.

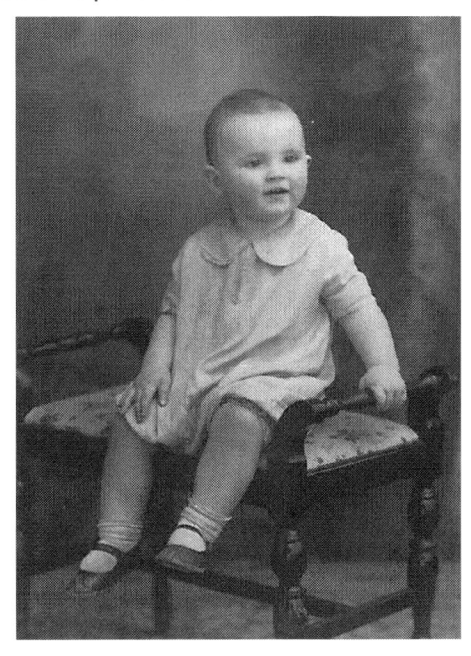

Owen Ness 1932(ish)

This happened a week before the inspection of the farm and all of its operations for a gold medal in comparison with other farms in the province of Quebec. The competition involved a silver medal competition in which a number of awards were made. Five years later, those winners could compete for the gold medal. Our farm won the gold medal that year (1935).

A by-product was a production of a complete report of the operations on the farm at that time. One of the interesting items was the total income of $7,200. At that time, we were six children and a hired man (although he only earned $30/per month plus room & board).

Other costs included operating tractor, truck, purchase of seed and fertilizer, and family living costs. We were probably considered to be wealthy.

back - Myrtle, John Earl, Jean, Elva, Robert Earle
front - Evelyn, Mildred & Owen MacGregor

My father was the only university graduate operating his own farm. He was a veteran of the First World War. When he graduated, his father asked him to take on the farm on which he owned a substantial mortgage and the farmer was about to go bankrupt. Many years later, when I started to draw a salary from Alcan, he was wondering out loud if he would not have been better off to have followed his classmates into business or government. I told him that I was glad that he had made the choice that he did. Five of the six children had gone to MacDonald College. Three of the girls were teachers, my brother took a two-year diploma course which was designed for people planning to farm. I had taken a degree course which eventually led to my only employment which was with Alcan.

I was very proud of my father because he was always a community leader. He was one of a small group of people who created the Barry Memorial Hospital in Ormstown which still operates today.

As Chairman of the local school board, he was able to convince the other members that they could afford top quality teachers. I benefited because Mr. King was Principal for three years while I was in grade 8,9 and 10. After the first year, three of the four other teachers in high school left for a variety of reasons. Mr. King told me later that he spoke to my father and told him what was happening, and Dad told him to go to MacDonald College, speak to the Dean to hire good teachers and to go to Bishops to hire an Assistant-Principal. Mr. King called Dad on the Friday night, told him that the Dean of the Teacher's School had recommended two of the best teachers ever to graduate in the many years that he had been there. The Dean had told him that if the little school in Howick would hire Doris Fraser and Jean Catterson for $950 a year, it would teach a lesson to the board of MacDonald school.

Mr. King later obtained a Masters degree from Columbia University, was Principal of Ormstown High School and later was Principal in a school on West Island.

After teaching for three years at Howick, Doris Fraser went on to post-graduate studies and eventually held three doctorate degrees from Harvard. She came to a fifty-year reunion and told about another role in a group of representatives of the fifty United States where she represented the State of Massachusetts.

Jean Catterson also took post-graduate studies and amongst other roles held a senior position in the Province of Quebec, Education Ministry.

Mr. Farquharson, the Vice-Principal, later became principal and eventually was Principal of one of the larger schools on West Island. I have always believed that the education which I received from these people was as good as anyone could hope for in a public school financed by the local farm community.

When I was in grade 9, the staff decided that we should learn about democracy. They organized the Student Council election. Grade 8 and 9 elected a candidate and grade 10 and 11 elected their candidate. I was genuinely surprised that I was chosen by my classmates.

Owen and Robert Bruce Ness

In the election which ensued, the staff decided there was a tie vote, we had election speeches. As I thought about what I should say,

I realized that grade 7 who also had a vote would probably determine the winner. As a true politician, I directed my promises to them, suggesting they should have more involvement in noon activities. We all travelled to school, in school buses, and after eating our sandwiches, we rushed out to play various sports during the remainder of the noon hour break.

The results of the election left Mr. King and the staff with me as President of the Student's Council. That may not have been what they expected.

Mr. King would take me out of classes for 15 to 20 minutes. He taught me how to structure my council and then taught me my first basic lessons in human relations. He had me read Dale Carnegie's "How to Win Friends and Influence People". He went through it part by part to point out the elements which were manipulative and emphasized the basic message of listening to people and understanding what they were saying.

In early February 1945, the older part of the school burned down on a Saturday night. I remember it well because I was taking a new girlfriend to skate on the open-air rink behind the school. When we arrived, the firemen were already there and succeeded in saving the newer part of the school. This meant that we had to get by with very cramped quarters for the rest of the time that I was at the school.

The Student's Council organized community dances and other events during the summer to raise money to replace sports equipment and other things which had been lost. I recently found a letter which Mr. King wrote to me during the summer. I don't remember receiving it but I was quite proud to read it.

The following year, the staff created a new body called the Citizen's Council which was essentially a self-discipline organization. It was only a partial success. At an evening meeting, the details of which I don't really remember but apparently, I got a little bit snooty. When Mr. King reprimanded me, I got even worse and said perhaps I should resign.

The next morning, Mr. King took the history class as the moment to give me the worst dressing down and even worse than I thought he was capable of doing. He essentially said that he didn't care if I wanted to under-perform and enjoy myself, but he would not accept the fact that I was disrupting the class in particular, my cousin. He said, "it's easy for you to get by, but when you talk to your cousin who has to work much harder and disrupt him, I will not accept it".

I had averaged 65% in the Easter exams and exceeded 80% in the year-end exams.

My cousin, Clifford Reddick, was at the center of two very interesting events. He lived farther along the road where the school bus picked us up. One morning as we were getting on the bus, he got off to deliver something to my mother. As he past the bus in front, a car carrying other school kids side-swiped him. Most of us on the bus saw it and we all remember it.

Lionel Upton, our Phys Ed and Elementary Trades teacher, found some boxing gloves and decided that we should learn how to box. After some rudimentary coaching, he decided that my cousin and I should be in the first match. We were in grade nine at that time and Clifford was already three inches taller than I was. To say that I was terrified, would be an understatement. As we got close to each other, I unleashed the biggest punch that I could muster - hit him on the nose, provoked a big nose bleed and that was the end of boxing in the school.

MY FIRST DAY ON THE JOB

On 26th of May 1954, I went to work for my first day on the job in Arvida for Alcan. The office was locked. It was located over the police station, so I went down and asked why the offices were closed. "Bien Monsieur, c'est la fête de l'Ascension et c'est un jour de congé pour tout le monde, sauf nous autres". I had a holiday for my first day!!!

The next day, I started my career with Alcan. The initial job was vaguely described but was only supposed to last for two years. The company had a serious problem caused by fluoride emissions from the smelters. We knew that dairy farms were suffering damages but had to intensify research on the problem at the same time as we looked for solutions on the damages. My job was to aid in research, evaluate the damages and later to create an experimental farm.

Many years later, I realized that my lead professor, Dr. E. W. Crampton, at MacDonald College, while acting as a consultant to Alcan, convinced the company that they should have someone with an agricultural background dealing with farmers. They also specified someone who was bilingual and understood research. I realized the importance of this when I saw the behaviour of American companies who dealt with the problem with chemists and lawyers.

At the first meeting with one of the farmers and their union representatives, we met at the house of Georges Jean whose farm was in the main area of damages.

Naturally, the Agronome (Agricultural Specialist) wanted to know more about this young English speaking guy who had suddenly appeared on the scene. I told them that I had my degree from MacDonald College and had continued on to seek a Masters degree. Unfortunately, my French failed me on occasion and I said mistress rather than master "maîtresse au lieu de maître". I had just accidentally broken the ice on a very positive 12-year relationship with the union (Union Catholique des Cultivateurs – UCC.; now called UPA, Union des Producteurs Agricoles).

Owen - Lab - Post Graduate Research

We had to examine the cows affected by the problem to find out their degree of exposure by examining their teeth. The teeth represented a record of the level of exposure to fluorides.

A small amount of fluoride is required to have strong teeth and bones. This formula is part of the fluorapatite ($Ca_5(Po_4)_5 F$) which is the main component of the bones and teeth. Slightly higher levels of additional Fluoride makes the molecules become chalky. This results first in dark staining of the teeth, then the teeth wear away. This was thought to be the cause of the animal's becoming much thinner but subsequent research showed that the thinness came from the effect on an enzyme essential to the releasing of the energy in the food.

The union had a veterinary acting as their advisor. In the Chicoutimi area, hIs reports were essentially identical to mine.

The veterinary in the region of the Ile Maligne plant produced very inaccurate reports because he never took off his tie and put on his overalls to examine the herd. One farmer said that he stood at the door and counted the cows.

I had a wonderful man, René Prevost, who worked with me in finding solutions to pay the damages. By law, damages were prescribed after two years. He came up with a formula whereby we gave four years past damages in return for a five-year Servitude. In other words, nine times the annual damages, as best we could determine them. This gave cash amounts sufficient to allow the farmers to purchase unaffected property and dilute their feed sufficiently to avoid damages, if they wished to continue farming. In comparison to U.S. settlements, they were low cost because there were no legal costs except the notary.

When we presented our offer for the initial group of farms, the Union had their lawyer present. We had our inside lawyer and our independent lawyer. It was the last time we had lawyers on either side. After we had presented our offers, Maitre. Fradette asked for a recess which probably lasted 40 minutes. When he returned, he said "we think this is a very fair offer and it will allow the farmers the choice of expanding their farms or choosing another profession. The fact that Mr. Ness has presented these offers, give me further confidence that this is fair".

Many weeks later, I discovered that he had two brothers-in-law who regularly attended an auction sale of purebred cattle at my grandfather's farm, some of which were imported from Scotland. The farm slogan was "our reputation is your guarantee". That seems to be where he had developed his judgement about me.

That block of settlements was for a group of farms near Chicoutimi for less than one million dollars. Some questioned why we were spending millions of dollars to correct the problem at the smelter. Senior management in Montreal rejected that idea.

When we addressed the problem around the Île Maligne smelter, I wrote a request for authorization for approximately $500,000. In the request, I asked that the approval be given before January and February because it was easier to deal with the farmers at that time.

Mr. Nathaniel Davis, Chairman of the Board, wrote a letter saying quite clearly that if this timing was to allow us to take advantage of our neighbours, he would not sign it. He went on to say that as long as he had been with the company, and as long as he was the Chairman of the Board, he would never approve an action which took advantage of our neighbours. To me, that was a statement of the values that he set for Alcan, which I always cherished.

Alcan was a member of a group of companies and government organizations, I think there were fourteen in all, which was sponsoring research to try to understand more thoroughly the effects of fluoride poisoning on cattle. The largest projects were at the University of Wisconsin and the University of Utah.

Although I did not get my Masters degree, according to my lead professor because I had screwed up a question on the biology of fluoride, I was elected head of the technical group overseeing the research at the two institutions. This was because all of the other companies were represented by lawyers and chemists. Fluoride poisoning was a problem around phosphate mining, aluminum smelters and in one case, a huge steel plant which was built in the middle of some of the richest farm land in Utah. No one had realized that the ore which they were using contained fluoride. Their law suits went on for years and years. There was probably no way that they could have used our approach.

A clear comparison of our approach was a small smelter in Troutdale, Oregon where the lawyers took the attitude of "we'll show them". They had a chance to settle with a farmer across the road from the smelter for $75,000. They eventually paid $1.2 Million dollars plus all of the legal costs.

In our case, we could not have found twelve people between Port Alfred and Roberval to form a jury, who could have understood the technical arguments if we had tried to go the legal route in dealing with our problem.

My job grew quite quickly.

Because I had an Agricultural degree, I found myself in charge of the Landscape Department, although I had no Horticultural training. Later, I was involved in acquiring rights of way for the Chute-des-Passes power lines, which crossed farm land and the Île Maligne switching station.

I am sure that I met with more farmers and their wives in their houses than any other English-speaking representative of the company. When we bought the right of ways, René Prevost and I were usually accompanied by the Notary, Victor U. Larouche.

The Landscape Department was a tremendous learning experience because we were covered by the Union agreement. At one point, the Vice-President responsible for our employees approached me and said that people opted for the plant when we were hiring for both the plant and the Landscape Department in the spring time because we worked our men too hard. For some reason, he never got around to confirming his request.

Landscape workers cut the grass, planted flowers and a variety of similar tasks.

Owen & Arlie – Prom, MacDonald College

MY SEVENTEEN YEARS IN THE SAGUENAY

I was employed in Arvida for eighteen years with one year out to go to CEI. The evolution of my tasks was interesting. Mr. Ted Eberts was my boss for the first two years, followed by Alton Locke. When Mr. Locke retired, Claude Aubin came from Montreal to replace him.

Ted had quite an imposing stature and a voice which went with it. We developed an excellent relationship as time went on. One incident was related to his love of gardening and his interest in the large landscape department for which our department was responsible. I was superintendent because I was a graduate in Agriculture, although I never took any horticulture classes. He came in one morning, having walked to work as usual, and said that we should collect all of the leaves from around our properties to add to our compost heaps. These were already quite extensive and were used in the gardens which we maintained. Rather than engage in an argument about the economics of such an action, I chose to go the route of the inappropriateness of dead leaves because we would be adding nothing but carbon, as compared to green material which still retained the potash and potassium residues which were essential to good compost. He listened, then said "oh hell, you know all about that, so we'll forget it".

In spite of his gruffness, Ted was a very kind and thoughtful person. We all saw this at his going away party where he demonstrated his passion for the Saguenay by crying during his thank you speech.

Shortly after taking responsibility for the Landscape department, Captain Zourro reported that my Foreman and General Foreman were using our skeleton winter crew to cut trees on the west side of the Shipshaw Power House and selling the logs. I very innocently asked him what I should do, but he said, "they will have to be terminated".

When I started the procedure, Mr. Eberts had a visit from the local priest who made the point that Alcan was considered to be a very generous company dealing with employees. To be terminated would leave these men as unemployable criminals in the eyes of the community. With the agreement of J.J. Gagnon, the Works Personnel Manager, Misters Dallaire and Bernier were given hourly paid employment in the Works and completed their working days there.

My principal responsibilities were, of course, dealing with the damage claims from the dairy farmers affected by the fluoride problem. We were co-sponsors with a large group of American companies on the research being done at the Universities of Utah and Wisconsin, and the Boyce Thompson Institute which specialized on studies of damage to vegetation.

We had damage to vegetation near the plant caused by hydrocarbons and in one case chlorine. I had the frightening experience of discovering that chlorine problem. We had large gulleys running to the Saguenay from various parts of Arvida Works. Some of these went into one large one and discharged various chemicals from the Works.

We had observed a swath of damage running from the gulley through the north western part of the town. I followed the damage to the gulley and very foolishly walked down into the gulley and got a whiff of what was close to pure chlorine. What had happened was that chemicals from different parts of the plant had interacted where there was about a ten-foot drop in the gulley and the chlorine was the product of that interaction. Needless to say, the problem was corrected very quickly. This was one of the factors which caused the company to set about correcting all of the problems from the multiple chemical products being produced in various parts of the plant.

The Boyce Thompson Institute did further research for Reynolds Aluminum Company when they got into litigation with a neighbouring farmer, assuming that they could reach a reasonable settlement. The litigants threw everything in the book at them, claiming vegetation damage, "sub-acute human ailments" and anything else of which they could think. This also provoked a research project at the Kettering Institute in Cincinnati which was rather strange because they had to decide the meaning of "sub-acute" human damage.

Before my arrival in Arvida, some thought had been given to creating an experimental farm to follow-up local conditions. We finally did this in 1957, made a lot of studies in the following six or seven years and it was eventually closed in the late '60s. Dr. Crampton and Dr. Dale from MacDonald College were our principal consultants.

We purchased a working farm and made very few changes, except to upgrade the herd of cattle to help cover the costs of operation. This turned out to have an excellent influence in developing a relationship with the local dairy farmers, many of whom were adopting new practices, including improving their herds. The farm manager insisted on competing at local agricultural fairs.

Having their animals come higher in classes than Alcan was a real feather in their cap.

I learned to respect our farm manager who had had another farm on his own, closer to the plant. He was working as a Foreman in the Île Maligne Plant and the Works Manager complained that we were taking one of his best people. We had to buy a new tractor and one month after it arrived, I visited the farm and the front end was against one wall of the garage, the other part was at the other side. I probably over reacted but Mr. Lavoie and his son showed me a broken part in the transmission which probably would have cost five weeks to have repairs from the agent. They were able to get the part in a few days and the following week were out plowing.

The dug well which we had on the farm was not sufficient to meet our needs, so we decided to dig a new well. After a number of attempts, including the local tradition of bringing in a water finder with his divining rod, Mrs. Lavoie who always resented moving from her old home in Range 1 to Range 3, said to me "I could have told you that a few feet down in this part of Range 3, it's all granite and there is no way you will get water". We solved the problem by putting in a water line to a farm half a kilometer away.

I believe our success in maintaining excellent relationships with our claimants was due to a number of factors, and Georges Henri Lavoie as our farm manager, made a tremendous contribution to this success. He was a graduate of l'École Moyenne d'Agriculture in Chicoutimi. Their teachings were what one would call, organic farming but the good farmers working with each other were upgrading their operations. An example of this was the teaching that it was harmful to the soil to take more than one crop of hay in one season. With the long days of sunshine at that latitude, it was easy to have three good crops in one season.

The farm was located on Île d'Alma. The main outflow from Lac St.-Jean was on the north side, and the smaller one was on the south. They were naturally called La Grande Descharge and La Petite Descharge.

The multi-billion dollar smelter which Alcan built almost two decades ago is on Île d'Alma, located as close as possible to the power houses on the Peribonka River which flows into Lac St.-Jean.

The last power house which was built was at Chute des Passes and my agricultural background led to my involvement in purchasing the rights of way in about fifteen miles of the southern end of the transmission lines and the purchase of the site for the large switching station. This was an interesting experience. The real negotiator was René Prevost and when we met with farmers, we always had the notary with us.

Our notary was Victor Ulderich Larouche, usually referred to as V.U. He lived in the small village of St-Coeur-de-Marie on the North side of Lac St.-Jean. He had an incredible memory and could tell you the phone numbers at noon of all the calls he had made in the morning. What was much more important was that he had complete command of Notarial law. He contributed tremendously to my understanding of the unique society in the Lac St.-Jean region.

Victor and René became close friends. It was always fun to listen to whether or not we were going to stop at Victor's house for a glass of Black & White before we went home. I always knew we would end up at Victor's house. This was where I really began to understand French innuendo. Both of them had a tremendous sense of humour.

Sometimes, we walked the area that we were planning to purchase. I don't remember where it was, but René and I went out on a cold, wet day in the Autumn. In early afternoon, we went to the notary's house, where I learned of another interesting local custom. I was introduced to a "Ponce" which is mostly Geneva gin and some other ingredient with hot water. It does warm one up.

When René was transferred to other responsibilities, I was assisted by another person, but I had the lead job. One evening before going to one of the farm houses, we decided to let my assistant do the negotiations. After we left, he asked the notary how he thought he'd done. The notary said "I would have to give you a very low mark. When we first started, the wife was quite sympathetic to what we were offering. You did not pick that up and by the time we left, it was clear that she would not support any deal with us." Naturally, I learned from all these incidents.

One of the interesting stories was our relationship with Elzebert Larouche. Shortly after we started our meeting with him, the notary turned to René and me and said, "no deal tonight". It was obvious that Elzebert had already enjoyed a couple. We naturally stayed for a while and visited with him. The next day, the notary said to Elzebert "tu dois demander la pardon de M. Ness. Tu l'as insulté hier soir". Elzebert wanted to know why he should apologize. The notary said, " in our conversation last night, you kept referring to les 'moadits blokes'. M. Ness est un bloke." We eventually completed a satisfactory deal, it was a fairly large purchase, including 50 acres of land for the Switching Station.

Later on, when construction of the station began, our resident engineer obtained quotations from various contractors to clear the site. Mr. Larouche who did contracting work for the paper companies in the forests, gave a quotation of $800 per acre. Our engineer refused it because he said it was far too low and granted the contract to a larger contractor operating out of Arvida. After one week, that contractor bought his way out of the contract because he couldn't see how he could break even at $5000 an acre. The engineer who claimed to be an expert because of experience in Kittimat asked me to talk to Mr. Larouche and find out how he was going to do it. The land was quite swampy and the plan to burn the material even with large quantities of tires did not work.

When I saw Mr. Larouche, he laughed and said "I knew you would be back, but I think I'll charge a little bit more. For $1000 per acre, I will do the job". I asked if he would mind telling me his secret, he said " I will strip off all of the shrubs and trees, bulldoze them over to my land and fifteen years from now, I will burn it".

This was one of the many experiences which led me to respect the large number of French Canadians who belong to a category which I call "le gros bon sens". They are very inventive and had a lot of common sense. The number of millionaires in Beauce County is a manifestation of this. Unfortunately, there is also a large part of our French-Canadian community who are more comfortable with bureaucracy.

One of the reasons that we took a notary with us was an incident which occurred on a previous project which René Prevost experienced. They purchased land for access to a powerhouse called Chute à la Savane on the Peribonka River. They completed a deal with the farmer and when they returned with the notary, the farmer denied any knowledge of what had been done. They nonetheless got an agreement and paid for it, but when the construction people arrived at the gate, he met them with a shotgun. Legal procedures were taken but it was also established when he tried to commit suicide that he should be sent to the mental institute near Quebec. Two police officers were transporting him to Quebec and they stopped for lunch at l'Étape. This was the only restaurant in the eighty-mile trip through the national park. They weren't paying much attention and suddenly noticed that their ward was running across the lake. In spite of his recent suicide attempt, they called out "Ârretes ou on tire". Fortunately, he stopped and came back.

As a part of the Chute-des-Passes Power House Project, Alcan built a village for the staff needed to operate the plant. I had two interesting experiences in relation to the village. They needed soil to cover what was essentially rocky land and turned to me to find the soil to be able to have lawns around the houses. I had taken a course in physical geography in high school and remembered that fine soil was usually deposited in the delta where one river runs into the other. I studied detailed maps and discovered a small river flowing into the main stream a few miles from the village. It turned out to be excellent soil.

The second Chutes-des-Passes experience was a few years later when I had changed careers. I had worked with numerous professors in team building exercises. The Power Division Personnel Manager organized a team building exercise for the seven teachers in the village school. Originally, I was to work with a professor from the University of Montreal. At the last minute, he advised us that he was not available, and the Personnel Manager insisted that I could do it myself. As it was only a group of seven, I agreed to do it. We got together for dinner on the Friday night, started our next session early the next morning. Around 11:00 a.m., Mr. Dufour called me from Arvida Works and said that he needed me urgently. I did not argue with him because I never won an argument when he said something was important.

I told the ladies that I would be back shortly after lunch to resume our session. When I returned, I asked them what they had been discussing. One of them said "Monsieur Ness, tout est reglé. On a fait pleuré la principale, après ca, nous avons reorganisé nos postes". Having observed the discussions the night before, I agreed entirely with what they had done. The Principal gave up her position and became responsible for grade two and music. The grade three teacher replaced her as Principal. All the ladies agreed to the change.

The former Principal was the wife of the Power House Superintendent. The new Principal was the wife of the Union President. I suppose one could have expected when staffing the school, it may have appeared obvious to have the two ladies in their original positions. In the discussions the previous evening it was obvious to me that the new principle was the natural leader of the group.

I met one of the ladies, twenty years later and she said that they had been a wonderful team until the school was closed. The company discovered that it was easier to fly in maintenance people and provide rooms for them rather than try to maintain a village.

Another interesting experience occurred when we were meeting with the farmers who had made claims and did not distinguish between the small ones and the large ones. A Mr. Joe Savard had made a claim, although he only had one cow. In his claim, he claimed that he lost a calf and in the following year, he had lost a yearling. I asked him if the cow had had twins in the previous years and he replied in the negative. On the way back to Chicoutimi with the Union representative, he asked me why I had asked that question. I said, "it was obvious, it couldn't die again in the following year".

On Alma Island, Range 3, there were nine farms. The average number of children was sixteen. Twelve alive. Mr. and Mrs. Armand Jean at the West end of the road had twenty-three children.

This brings back to mind, the level of poverty which I saw in some of those homes. Including one or two owners who signed the documents with an "x". At the Cauchon farm, we saw the bread man come in with what appeared to be a dozen loaves of bread, and I was told that supper that night would probably be bread and melted sugar.

Ten years later after the settlement, three of the sons were working in the smelter. The father had purchased two other farms and had brought the whole family to a state of relative comfort.

THE MOST IMPORTANT YEAR OF MY LIFE

September 1960-1961

In 1937 the United States Government subjected the Aluminum Company of America to an antitrust action because Alcoa owned most of the aluminum operations in the United States and elsewhere.

The result of the action left Alcoa owning everything in the United States and the company called Aluminium Limited owning everything in the rest of the world. The Canadian operations were by far the largest of this company.

With the Second World War the demand for aluminum was enormous. The British government loaned millions of dollars to the Canadian company known as Alcan. It was loaned at a rate of 2% repayable by 1972. With this money Alcan built power houses in Lac St-Jean and at Shipshaw on the Saguenay river and expanded their smelter to become the biggest in the world.

With the end of the war Alcan had this capacity without any obvious market.

The chairman of the board amongst other policies decided that Aluminum Limited through Alcan had to become the most international company in the world. He made policies which included creating an international business school in Geneva, Switzerland. The school was called Centre d'Études Industriales (CEI).

The school opened in 1947 with 30 students. This was the size throughout its life. The class was selected entirely from existing or newly hired employees. Over the years this was changed to a mix of employees from other companies in other countries.

In the spring of 1960 I saw a brochure indicating the qualifications for employees who might wish to participate in the program. I had the necessary academic qualifications.

I walked across the street in Arvida to talk to Bohdan (Bob) Hawrylyshyn. He had been a student at CEI two years earlier. I told him that I wanted to apply to attend the school. He laughed at me. "You have never been inside the plant and I can name five or six people who are more likely to be named than you".

Subsequentially I learned that there were 53 candidates. Bob coached me on my application and at different steps of the process. A committee of senior managers interviewed all of the candidates. Bob said that their task was to select those that were most likely to stay with Alcan. My boss gave me a surprisingly laudatory recommendation.

When it came time for the interview he said they want to know how much you know about the company. He said "Read the last three annual reports". The secretary of the committee later on said that I was the most knowledgeable person about Alcan that they had ever interviewed.

About three months later I was advised that I had been selected with two others of the 53 who had applied.

On September 10th Arlie and our three children embarked with me on the SS Homeric, an Italian ship which sailed out of Montreal. When we arrived at 'Le Havre' Port in France we then took the train to Paris. Reservations had been made in a hotel. While I went to get tickets for the train to Geneva, Switzerland Arlie was all alone for about four hours. She did not appreciate being in the center of Paris, no money and no idea what to do if I didn't come back.

We took the train in the evening and arrived in Geneva at midnight. When I got off the train, I suddenly asked myself 'what am I doing to my three boys and my wife'? It turned out alright over the following twelve months. In less than one week, with the help of an agent, we found a house in a small village outside Geneva. It belonged to a couple from Haiti. I don't know if it was their home or simply an investment in a safe country. It was very comfortable with a view from the bathroom of Mont-Blanc.

David went to first grade at the local village school and Peter went to 'enfantine' (kindergarten). They did very well. One of the teachers commented that they were speaking French in five weeks while the Swedish and American children who lived in a closed community had made very little progress.

Bruce was three years old and spent his days with his mother. He was slow to speak. He would say things like mamma, let's go chez-nous.

Arlie spoke little French but managed to make friends with one of the village ladies, Mme. Monod, who taught her the many ways to use cabbage since that was the cheapest vegetable.

Arlie had to get a Swiss licence although she didn't have a Quebec licence at the time. Amongst the tests was the ability to back up into a parking spot on the side of a hill.

There were many one way roads in the mountains where the car going up the hill had to let the other car pass.

One of the questions referred to the word 'freins', a truck driver told her it is 'brakes' madam. There were many situations where I admired how Arlie constantly dealt with difficult situations.

It would take a number of pages to describe the things that we did away from school.

At CEI courses were designed to meet our needs as compared to a normal Master's Degree where many other things were included that were not necessarily of value going into business. The professors were mostly invited from European Universities. Two of the staff members had been professors at Harvard. We had businessmen make presentations of certain aspects of their business. Some of the class presented lectures on subjects with which they were familiar.

Everyone had to present a thesis on something which we had studied. Doctor Paul Haenni, the principle of the school told me to study the teachings of 'Malthus' who had written various papers about the world running short of food. The conclusion of my thesis was that the world could supply plenty of food but would likely have problems because of politics.

My Classmates

Since it was an international school, the students were an international group. We had four Canadians, three Americans, one Venezuelan, three Swedes, one Dane, one Belgian, one Frenchman, one Italian, three Indians, two Africans and two Japanese, the remainder were from the U.K.

Successful Classmates

Adolf Lundin created the Lundin mining company based in Calgary, Alberta because it was better than most places for financing his type of operation. Created in the seventies, the company is still operating in many countries.

David Morton became chief executive officer of Alcan in 1988.

A third classmate from Switzerland became the head of CibaGeigy, a Large Swiss company.

I think I was successful.

Why Geneva?

The school was located in Geneva, Switzerland because it was almost the center of Europe. It was a tri-lingual country; the League of Nations was located there which made it an international city.

Why the 'Most' Important year of my Life?

The position which I held in 1961 had become much less important because of the successful settlements which we had made and the improvements to control the effluents from the works.

All of the positions above me were lawyers. I had no plant-operation experience and most of them were engineers or chemists.

Two months before I was transferred to Arvida works I applied for a position in Ottawa but the department in Ottawa decided that they needed someone with a Doctorate degree.

Without the experience and learning at CEI I would not have had the qualifications to move up in the company.

David and Peter's health problems dictated a move to Montreal which opened up possibilities in the international activities of the company. Initially I was in charge of compensation policies. This led to working with Latin-America and when the manager of Latin-America moved to the head office I became vice president of personnel for his group of companies which included Europe, Africa and Latin-America. After four years of travelling I took the job in England with David Morton which is described further later on in the book.

The personnel mandates which I had between 1966 to 1993 would have been very difficult for me if I had not had an extensive training in dealing with people. I was able to develop positive relations with the many countries and people with whom I dealt as I assumed more and more senior responsibilities.

Bohdan (Bob) Hawrylyshyn

My decision to consult Bob on my application to participate in the CEI program turned out to be very wise. I did not know that he was about to be transferred permanently to CEI.

Bob's career after he went to CEI was entirely as a professor on many subjects. As the years went by he was awarded seven honourable doctorates amongst several other awards. The information on his career in Wikipedia is astonishing.

After the breakup of the Soviet Union Bob went home to the Ukraine where he spent the rest of his life but stayed active in Europe and North America.

ADRIAN PLOURDE

The Union Leader who Changed my Career

Adrian Plourde was a President of the union at Arvida for many years. I did not know him very well but when I was responsible for the Landscape Department, I had to replace the General Foreman. After interviewing a number of people, including farmers, I chose Mr. Antonio Dufour to take the position. Mr. Eberts, my boss, objected to the idea of hiring the union representative for the department to take the position. Mr. René Prevost had helped me with the interviews and we pointed out to Mr. Eberts that Mr. Dufour had won the large majority of the grievances filed against us.

Mr. Antonio Dufour was one of the founders of the union and he talked of following the gulley through the town to get to the school house where they held their meetings. He was the first person to tell me about Mr. Plourde and his abilities as a leader.

Mr. Gaston Dufour (no relation to Antonio Dufour) was the Works Manager of Arvida Works, the largest smelter in the world at that time, with over six thousand workers.

Mr. Plourde showed his statesmanship when he approached Mr. Gaston Dufour in January 1966. The conversation went like this: Mr. Plourde, "We have to change our way of dealing with each other. Having my members walk off work every time the company wants to reduce manpower is the wrong way to approach the modernization which is needed to keep the company competitive."

I suggest that we create a committee to study how to make changes without it being on the backs of the workers (sur le dos des travailleurs). My five Vice-Presidents would be on the committee and you would name your representatives.

When they arrive at solutions, the company will take responsibility to implement the changes. My Vice-Presidents must retain their "role revendicateur". (This meant that he did not want them to forget that they were representing the members).

Mr. Dufour " this is the best idea I have heard in the eighteen months that I have been in the position. We should try to make this work".

Mr. Dufour then consulted with Mr. Mackenzie, General Superintendent of the Reduction Division and some of the other superintendents. He then spoke to Mr. Dick Fortier, Personnel Manager and told him that he could name four of the five people that the company would have, but he would select the fifth person.

I was the fifth person and Mr. Dufour had chosen me because he had been Works Manager at Ile Maligne when we settled the farmers' claims around that plant. He knew that we had achieved excellent relationships with the farmers and their union. In fact, we did not have lawyers on either side of the settlement of the problems.

In his years, as Manager of Ile Maligne Works, Mr. Dufour had become a part of the community and knew many of the business leaders around Alma, hence his thorough understanding of what I'd been doing.

The Research Committee on Change was chaired by Hugues Leydet, who was the Head of Labor Relations at that time. As Personnel Superintendent in the Reduction Division, I was the primary link to the operations where most of the changes were to take place.

As with all good studies, we looked at the statistics of the Works population in Arvida. We discovered that there were more than 400 out of 6,000 employees "hidden" in the Works. Many of them were called Janitors - most of them were not able to do the work that was available. We also realized that most of the workers had been recruited during or right after the war, and we were approaching a very high natural attrition rate.

The solution, to making changes acceptable to the workforce, was to create an early retirement program which was quite justified because very few of these men were going to reach the age of 65, and benefit from the pension plans to which they had paid for most of their working days. These pensions were funded outside the regular pension fund.

Since most of the job reductions were in the top paying jobs, we provided maintenance of earnings for up to six months. Very few of these were needed because of the attrition rate.

There were 24 Soderberg lines and each operating shift had seven crew members. These were the highest paying jobs with the workers who had the highest seniority. As a result of the changes in operation, the crews were reduced to six crew members per shift. The loss of ninety-six of the top paying jobs was very significant to the workers who had to work many years to achieve that level.

The Research Committee was a very new approach to solving problems. Custom was to negotiate whether both parties knew the solution or not.

When we were close to agreeing, the crews who replaced the anodes, walked off work at midnight one night. They were a completely different group from the Cell Operators and normally worked day shifts. We were expanding the production of each reduction cell by widening the cells, That meant that the anodes were consumed more quickly and the anode changers had to change to 24-hour shifts. When Mr. Leydet, Head of Labour Relations, was advised of the walk-out, he called in the security forces and made sure that all of the affected men left the plant. I thought he was crazy but then I realized that the "pot workers" were all on 24-hour shifts and wouldn't follow the smaller group out in the walk-out.

Mr. Plourde was in Baie Comeau settling some problem with the Reynolds Aluminum workers who were a part of his union. He came back to Arvida and met with Mr. Dufour and Mr. MacKenzie, the General Superintendent of the Reduction Division. Shortly after the meeting started, Mr. Dufour came to my office and said "Mr. Plourde wants Arvida to be like the Port of Antwerp, not like the Port of Rotterdam. Owen you have been to Europe, what's he talking about?" I said it was simple, the Port of Rotterdam had very poor operations while the Port of Antwerp which had been modernized with the collaboration of the unions, was the most efficient port in Europe. I added that the Port of London was in the same category as Rotterdam. Ironically, Mr. Plourde and all of his vice-presidents had visited Europe and were half a step ahead of most of our plant management.

Mr. Plourde asked how we had communicated these changes to the effected workers. Mr. MacKenzie said that the decision was made by the superintendents working with him. Then the communication went down the line to the supervisors, the General Foreman, the Shift Foreman who advised the workers. Mr. Plourde asked if they were aware that the workers from three pot lines shared the same lunch rooms. He said that the workers then discussed what they had heard and tried to decide what the real message was.

As a result of these discussions, we agreed with the Union to do something radically different. We paid the men for two hours extra after their shift and held meetings to explain the changes and how they would be affected. The Union Vice-President for the Division attended all these meetings. At the first meeting, the workers had decided not to get drawn in by this process and that they would not ask questions. We were perhaps half way through the two hours when one of the workers stood up and said that he wasn't going to participate in the boycott. This immediately opened up a general discussion which turned into a discussion with the Union Vice-President about everything that was bothering them, because such a general meeting rarely occurred. Subsequent meetings became similar open forums.

We learned some lessons about organizing such meetings. Do not hold them during the Stanley Cup and do not hold them after the night shift when the men wanted to get to bed as soon as possible.

We implemented a change one pot room at a time. After about three successful changes, Mr. Dufour asked me if I was planning to take a holiday at Easter. He knew that we usually took the boys out of school and went to Florida for 10 days. He said "you can't go this year because the changes will not be completed. The Union would inevitably come up with some demands in return for having agreed to these changes". I told Mr. Dufour that this was not an ordinary agreement because we had met directly with the employees. There was no evidence of any disagreement and the changes had already been effected, in part of the plant.

We could legitimately claim that we had negotiated directly with the workers because of the meetings at which they could express their views, not only to us but also to their union vice-president.

As a result of Mr. Dufour's claim that we should be prepared if something went wrong, we had identified some concessions which could be given.

When all of the changes had been completed, we realized that the things which we were willing to concede were of as much value to the company as they were to the workers.

For years in pot rooms everywhere, anode effects occurred frequently and had to be "killed". This was a thin layer of gas which formed on top of the bath and cut off the current and stopped the reduction process. They were corrected by breaking the crust mechanically. Everyone knew that the effects could also be killed by thrusting a piece of wood into the bath causing a minor explosion and correcting the problem. They were generally not allowed because there was a belief that the wood would introduce impurities into the metal.

I organized a meeting of the General Foremen and two Senior Supervisors to decide how to make these changes. The General Foremen thought we should just introduce the changes. The Senior Supervisors said that we should trade them for other things that were of value to the company. The principal change was to eliminate a large number of "ententes" which were agreements on different problems, but which were completely out of date.

LE PRESIDENT CAUSE FORMATION des adultes avec Mme Dorothy Pertuiset, les trois personnages du centre sont: MM. Owen Ness, le nouveau directeur des services du Personnel; Claude P.-Beaubien, vice-président, Relations publiques et Publicité de l'Alcan; et Pierre Hogue, qui partira en janvier pour la nouvelle usine de Lynemouth, en Angleterre.

The group arrived at an excellent consensus largely because the Senior Supervisors chose not to follow the easy solution.

Following these changes while Mr. Dufour and Mr. Plourde were still leading developments in Industrial Relations, we had an excellent period of positive relations leading up to the labour contract which was signed at the end of 1968. Mr. Plourde set the tone by setting a target of signing a contract before the previous one expired. This was achieved.

At the first negotiation meeting, he proposed to Mr. Leydet that he would present all of the Union demands and at the second meeting, the company would indicate which ones they would reject. There were over forty demands and I believe that Mr. Leydet refused more than thirty of them. Mr. Plourde only interrupted the listing to be sure that the company understood the demand.

Ironically, prior to the start of negotiations, our negotiating teams underwent a one-week training session. Mr. Paul Renaud was our principal "professor". He was one of the top labour relations lawyer in the province. The one lesson which he kept driving home was to make it very clear from the beginning of negotiations if there were demands which you intended to refuse, no matter where the negotiations went.

Mr. Plourde also made the change of the Union not making a monetary demand. In recent negotiations, the comparative companies were quite well established, so he did not see the value of a high Union demand and a low company offer, which inevitably arrived at the point that both parties knew from the beginning was the proper level.

Unfortunately, the company decided to change its policy in contract negotiations in 1973.

THE HUMAN SIDE OF ENTERPRISE

In a separate section, I have reported how the union president was responsible for my change from the Property Department to beginning a career as a professional "people" man.

From a job where I was involved in research and dealing with our neighbours on a host of problems, as well as managing the Landscape Department, I was suddenly plunged into one of the most exciting phases of Personnel Management ever seen in Alcan. This came about for several reasons. The teaching at CEI was in tune with the latest research and studies at Harvard. We made extensive use of case studies. This had led to the growth of almost all aspects of management training under a man named Alex Wynn. He had the support of many of the top managers and the general approach to people management was entirely in tune with the philosophy of Edward K. Davis.

This was also shortly after the publication of a book called "The Human Side of Enterprise". In the mid-60's with the support of Jim Cameron and other members of the smelter management, we began training sessions called "t-groups". These sessions usually lasted ten days; had forty participants, usually divided into groups of ten, and with the guidance of psychologists, learned about themselves and their ability to express their views to the people with whom they worked.

It used some of the methods of group therapy. A psychologist was present in all sessions.

This training was very controversial because some people experienced breakdowns. To my knowledge, most of them recovered and were left stronger people because they were able to get treatment.

Owen Ness 1967

In the group with which I spent the ten days, we did have one casualty. The sessions started, as I recall, early in the week and ran through until Wednesday of the following week. On the Sunday, I went out for a walk with four other participants. This session took place at the Hermitage Club which has a golf club on the edge of Lake Memphramagog.

At lunch time, someone came to me and said, "Ed wants to see you in cabin 2". When I got there, he was sitting on the stairs, soaking wet. This was the 5th of May and it was obvious that he had walked out into the lake before coming to his senses. He said to me "I don't know what I did". The psychologist took the case in hand and sent him to Montreal for professional care. He recovered completely, and his wife later said that it was a miracle that he had been able to get help when he really needed it. He continued with the company until normal retirement.

On our first sessions, on the following day, it was noticed that Ed was not with us. A discussion followed about what had happened in the Friday session, when some of Ed's conversation was not lucid. The biggest lesson that I learned was to find two members of the group who hadn't noticed Ed's struggles.

The company Chief Medical Officer in Arvida was strongly opposed to these training sessions because of the risks that he observed.

So-called "family groups" were then conducted on weekends where people who worked together would meet from Thursday noon until Sunday noon. A typical group would involve Production foremen with Maintenance and other service foremen where team work was imperative to achieve good results including Safety management.

Typically, in work groups over time, misunderstandings would grow into serious dislikes with the inevitable effect on team work.

As a Personnel professional most involved with "change programs", I was selected to work with psychologists who came from Harvard, University of Montreal and Laval University. It was the most intense internship that anyone could ever have had in what was essentially group therapy.

The doctor changed his mind completely about these group sessions after witnessing the changes in many of the men.

One General Foreman managed the crews which provided maintenance on the evening and night shift. This meant that he knew a large number of people and at one of our later sessions, he started out by saying "David et Charles, c'est le temps que tu te parle". He knew where there were bad relations between people for no good reason.

These groups were organized all the way up to senior management. The results were astonishing.

We had one group of General Foremen which began just after dinner. They were all so nervous that we literally had an average of three people talking at any one time for almost an hour and a half. At one point, I interrupted the conversation and thought that I had to put a little order into the proceedings. At the end of the session, I complimented myself to Dr. Sevigny. He simply said, "you do not know what would have happened if you hadn't interfered".

In 1967 or 1968, Hugues Leydet and Jean Mainville went to UCLA to learn about a program called Sociotech, which was the development of team work which led to more sophisticated multi-tasking and team work. At one point, ten of us went to UCLA to learn more about this approach.

When we applied these methods, the union worked with us because they saw this as a way of making work more interesting for their members and in some cases, brought better pay.

When I retired in 1993, 22 years after I left Arvida, Emery Leblanc invited me to visit the various plants in the Saguenay where this type of people development had reached new levels of success.

He had me visit eight different operations where Group Operations had led to great success. The one I remember most was the Laterrière Smelter which was still quite new. The casting plant had a problem cooling ingots. The metal has to be cooled very quickly when it is removed from the reduction cells.

The engineering people had designed a solution which would cost up to 3 million dollars and would take many months to get the necessary permits to use more water from the river.

Management put together a team of hourly paid workers to make recommendations as to what alternatives might be possible. The presentation which I attended was made by the workers. They had shown a way to use their water supply in a different way and came up with a solution which could be implemented immediately at a cost of fifty thousand dollars.

At one time, the person who was speaking said that they had the ideal team because they had an even mix of blues, reds and blacks, or some other combination of colours. I asked Evelyne Tremblay who was acting as my guide, what they meant. She said that all of these people had had rudimentary training in the psychological makeup of the ideal group which required different ways of approaching problems. The different colours signified different personality types.

MY ROLL OF HONOUR

Some would say that I have had a successful career. I started wearing coveralls and examining cow's teeth. I retired as Vice-President Personnel for the parent company. In terms of rank, one could also say that I went a long way up the ladder. I apologize for this digression, but I always think of promotional ladders in the terms of one of Alcan's Directors, who said "the view is never good when you look up the ladder and see what's above you".

The truth is that I had a great number of people who taught me the things I needed to know and/or demonstrated by their own behaviour the best way to do things.

Owen Ness 1968

My Family

I will start with my family. As I comment elsewhere in these memoirs, I was very fortunate to have a father who was the oldest in his family and a university graduate. To my knowledge, there was no one operating a farm in our area who had that level of education. He wholeheartedly contributed to the community, helped the neighbours to keep records and registrations of their purebred cattle, was an elder of the church, chairman of the school board and one of the founders of the Barry Memorial Hospital which still operates today. My brother Bobby, the hired man and I were always working with my father.

I thought that Dad was very tough on the men that we hired. I still remember old Tom Tomalty going to the milk train having been fired the night before. It was obvious that he was not able to do the heavier work which was required. This was not toughness but a case of facing the facts. We had to have able bodied help with the farm work.

I know I never showed my appreciation for Dad as much as I should have. The night I was in a public speaking competition and backed out at the last minute because I was not well enough prepared. He should have been angry at me, but if he was, he didn't show it.

He was quite upset when I accepted the job with Alcan at a monthly pay of $250. He said, "you have been through seventeen years of education and that's all they would pay you?"

At the visitation for his funeral, it suddenly hit me that he was my greatest fan and supporter. I can only hope that he was pleased with the road I took.

I was very fortunate to be the fifth of six children. Three girls, my brother, me and my younger sister. They were all supportive at different times and different ways. For instance, I remember the first time I played for the school hockey team and Bobby told me "don't ask the coach to put you on the ice; he has enough to think about without having the players tell him what to do".

I was closest to Elva, the second oldest of the girls because she was the best pianist and I had some ability to sing. We naturally talked to each other more than the others. I remember one day I told her I was afraid of something. She said "they won't kill you, will they"? I said, "of course not". It always made a difference in dealing with a problem.

We had a very happy family. My father was one of four brothers. All of them were farmers living within four miles of each other. This meant close relations with many cousins.

My grandfather had a very interesting and active life. He is alleged to have crossed the ocean over 40 times to purchase purebred dairy cattle and Clydesdale horses from Scotland. This was an unpredictable business, but he had more good fortune than set-backs. On one of the ships, there was a bull infected with tuberculosis and all the cows and heifers were affected. These cattle could still produce milk and healthy off-spring, so my father took them, and it became the basis of a very good herd.

Grandpa was a member of the Upper House in Quebec when the Senate still existed. There were a number of English speaking people involved in government at that time. The Order of Canada and the Order of Quebec did not exist in the late 30's but he was awarded a Member of the British Empire from the British government.

In his early 40's, Grandpa was sent home from the hospital in Montreal to die, allegedly because of a kidney disease. The local doctor disagreed and treated him for bleeding ulcers.

Owen and Bobby Ness

One of the treatments was to start smoking. I always remember him with a pipe or a cigar. He lived longer than anyone else in the family until Bobby surpassed him in 2016 at 89 years of age. The wooden arms on his arm chair had deep scratches where he lit his matches.

Eric King

From the time that the area around home was settled in the early 1800's, the Scottish community always put education first. As soon as they could build a school, they built it. Churches came much later.

The interest in education meant that the school board had tremendous support. For many years, the schools were "one room school houses". They were located in such a fashion that the children were within three miles walking distance. In the early 1930's, the first consolidation of schools, eliminated five or six one room school houses and created one school from elementary through high school. This was well ahead of many parts of Quebec and Eastern Ontario. When I started school in 1936, we travelled in a homemade school bus built and operated by local garages. In the winter, because the roads were not opened, we travelled in "sleigh buses", similar to the "prairie schooners". It did not happen often, but every once in a while, we thought it was fun to roll it on its side and our driver would stand beside the sleigh until we set it up again. Around 1937, the roads were opened throughout the winter and we were back to school buses year-round.

In early February, when I was probably in grade three, we had a very heavy snow storm and the school bus got stuck about a mile from the school. We sat and waited for help. I was sitting beside Phyllis Nussey who was in grade 11, probably because she was the prettiest girl I had ever seen. She was my first love. She tore a piece of paper out of one of her books and wrote an SOS note and we threw it out the window. That night, we had about ten children stay with us over night because the buses could not go any further than our farm.

We had good teachers, mostly graduates of MacDonald College and many of them became permanent residents as wives of local farmers.

This brings me to Mr. King. When I was in grade eight, Mr. Eric King who had taught in the Gaspé was hired as Principal of the Howick school. At the end of his first year, he lost all the high school staff except the teacher who taught French. Dad was chairman of the school board and Mr. King reported this to him. Dad told him to go to MacDonald College and see Dean Laird who had been head of the school for many years. Mr. King told the story that on the Friday night, he phoned Dad and said that Dean Laird had suggested that they hire Doris Fraser and Jane Catterson. The Dean said, they are amongst the best to ever graduate from Mac and he hoped that Howick could hire them but they would have to pay $950 a year. He wanted to show the MacDonald school which served Ste. Anne de Bellevue that a group of farmers would pay $50 more per year then their school would.

Mr. King told me later that Dad had succeeded in getting approval from the school board.

Doris Fraser taught for three or four years. She joined us at our fifty-year celebration. She had three Doctorate degrees, mainly from Harvard and was very active in politics as the representative of Massachusetts in a group where each state had one representative and constituted an independent think tank to provide guidance to the Federal government.

Jane Catterson also obtained a PHD, held a senior position in the Quebec Education Department, then moved out West.

At the same time, the school board hired Keith Farquarhson from Bishop's to be the Vice Principal. He eventually was a Principal of one of the large schools on the West Island.

I tell you all this background because it had a profound effect on my early education. The staff decided to teach us about democracy and organized a Student's Council election. Grades 7 through 11, had the vote. Grade 8 and 9 had to nominate a candidate, as did grade 10 and 11.

I am still surprised that I was the grade 9 candidate against the grade 11 candidate. A vote was organized, and the staff declared that it was a tie. We then had to make speeches to the high school's students. As usual, I was too lazy to prepare a learned address, but it was obvious to me that grade 7 had the controlling votes. As any good politician would do, I promised them more involvement in noon hour activities. I still haven't figured how I was going to do that. My opponent made a very nice speech describing all of the things that the Student's Council could do. Mr. King thus found himself with the kid from grade 9 as President of the Council. His response was to teach me how to manage, how to organize a Student's Council and conduct the meetings. A virtual business course. He took me out of classes for 15 minutes or so to teach me, but he also had me read "How to win friends, and influence people" by Dale Carnegie. This book was written in 1936 and today is still one of the best philosophy for anyone who has a management position.

The staff supported inter-scholastic activities with a number of schools in our own area, as well as Granby and other schools where Mr. King had personal contacts.

It was reported to him that there had been too much necking on the bus on the way home from Granby. He simply said, "you people should remember that there is a time and a place for everything". He didn't say whether the bus was one of them.

Many years after his retirement, I visited Mr. King. He told me that when Bobby was in grade 11, he asked him to clear the ice for the hockey game. He looked out later and saw Bobby and his friend, Murray Templeton, working away to clear the ice. Two weeks later, he gave me the same task and when he looked out, I was leaning on the boards, talking to a friend while six other kids were cleaning the ice. He told me that he had asked Dad if he knew his sons well. Dad said "as well as anyone could know their sons. We play softball together. We work together year-round including the summer time, during all the phases of growing and harvesting our crops".

They both agreed that I was lazy.

Math McKell

Math reminds me of one of the things that I learned about myself. He was in a generation before me, but he participated in one of two incidents when I learned that if I really lost my temper, the consequences could be frightening. The first incident occurred in a high school hockey game when I was in grade 11. The school was so small that we had to have everybody play who was able. When we played against Valleyfield, their Gault Academy, had a much larger enrollment.

I played the entire game by alternating between forward and defense. My defense partner, Raymond Cullen, made what I thought was a very legal sliding check but received a penalty. I "ragged " the puck, went around the net, shot the puck down the ice and "accidentally" flattened the guy who was coming at me. The referee who should have been an adult provided by the Valleyfield team was one of the members who would have been a player.

I saw him coming towards me with his arm raised to signal a penalty which of course would have left us three on five. I think I went in to what is called a "blind rage". I don't recall hitting him, but I did see him flat on the ice in front of me.

The other occasion was when the village team were playing against a town team from Valleyfield and one of their players hit Raymond Cavanagh, the smallest player on the team. I naturally had to defend my friend and got into a fight with that individual.

The game was played in the Ormstown arena which had been built for horse shows. The stands were about 10 feet above the ice surface. Math leaned down over the railing and shouted at me "give it to him, Owen, give it to him".

It wasn't the same blind rage as the first incident, but I did learn that I could be dangerous to myself.

I developed a special name for Math. On the Saturday morning of Havelock Fair, I was sitting too close to the porridge pot and had a porridge blister on my nose. Math saw me at the Fair and teased me about the nose. I called him Porridge Math anytime I saw him in the future.

My Westmount High Teachers And Friends

When I took my senior matriculation, grade 12 at Westmount High, we had excellent teachers, although I don't remember all of the names. Professor Schaffleburger was an excellent chemistry teacher.

"Squirt Smith" was our math teacher, on a part-time basis. He was a lawyer as his regular profession. I was walking up the stairs to our penthouse classroom after the Christmas break. We were walking side by side and he said out of the side of his mouth "Ness, you damn fool, if you don't smarten up, you're going to waste your year". That was my incentive to stop trying to commute the one-hour morning and night from the farm. I had fallen behind because I spent one week in November at the Royal Winter Fair competing in the dairy competitions, in an organization which later became the 4-H Clubs.

Shortly afterwards, I suffered a severe cut in my foot playing hockey and missed another four days. These were great excuses, but he did wake me up, and I managed to complete the year with only one supplemental exam.

Owen Ness, 1952

Late in the summer, I was able to take the supplemental exam at Sir George Williams College. Richie Lord was also taking the exam and he carried his desk over and set it beside mine. The invigilator who knew him came over and said "Richie, you know you can't do that". Richie replied, "my father always told me that the Lord helps them that helps themselves and I think Owen knows one or two answers".

I grew up out in the farming country where we almost never saw black people. In my class in Westmount there were probably three or four. Richie was my best friend because we had both played on the football team and we had also played together on the hockey team. We played on the same line and we had to kill the penalties. We won the Protestant Championship that year and in the city championship where we had to play regular hockey without any of the regulations against body checking. The City final was against Catholic High and one of their defensemen put Richie in the front row of seats in the forum.

Richie was awarded a hockey scholarship at the University of Michigan and completed his degree. He was very active in immigration matters and other political concerns of his neighbours in the St. Henri district of Westmount.

When we were in grade 12, people were suggesting that Richie had a gang in St. Henri. They always had some kind of a rumble on Queen Victoria Day. I asked him if he was the leader, what did he do? He said, "I get behind and push as hard as I can".

Mr. Patrick, our coach on the football team, told me that he was glad the season was over after the last game. I asked him why and he said, "you came through without a broken neck". I had never played football before and apparently my downfield tackles were very aggressive, and he thought I might get a broken neck.

FRIENDS, TEACHERS BOSSES & EMPLOYEES

As a student at MacDonald College, I had the benefit of a mature group of professors. They came from Ireland, the U.S., Switzerland, Trinidad Tobago and, of course, from Canada.

Dean Brittain held the position of Dean for most of the five years that I was on campus. He was very dedicated to MacDonald and was a creator of the Arboretum. His knowledge of trees left us an exhibit which would match almost anything in Eastern Canada. When I began my graduate studies, he offered me the position of warden for the Men's Residence. This task was almost totally dedicated to maintaining discipline amongst the residents.

I was quite taken aback because I was amongst the small group of "trouble makers". Nothing very damaging, for instance when Oleana Supreme, a famous purebred cow, in the college dairy herd passed away someone made a large Memoriam poster. She had produced more milk in her life time than any other recorded cows. We also hung the college flag at half-mast. Unfortunately, there was a freezing rain shortly afterwards. Someone sent the janitor to bring down the flag. Unfortunately, it was frozen to the cupola on the main building and was badly torn when he pulled it down. There was naturally a very serious enquiry, but the student's council ended up having to pay.

We also greased a 30-pound pig one night and released it in the women's residence. Unfortunately, it was during the winter time and the poor little thing was so cold that no one had to chase it.

I naturally accepted the job because it provided me with room and board which helped my budget immensely.

As I knew all of the trouble makers, I was able to keep things under control by designating which wing of the building could be used for parties.

When the diploma students had their graduation dinner, I stayed up until 3:00 a.m. and was quite sure that everything was under control. When I was walking to the cafeteria someone stopped me and said did you see the water tower, and there it was, DIP CLASS 53. It took me two months to find out that the two men who had done it were perhaps the quietest ones in the class.

Naturally, I had to report to Dean Brittain that the tower had been painted. He was very upset and claimed that this had never happened before. I interrupted him and said, "my uncle painted that tower in 1928". He said, "what tower are you talking about". I said," the big water tower". He said, "Oh hell, they have a responsibility to paint that". He had thought that I was talking about the cupola on the top of the main building.

In 2014, I met one of the perpetrators and he told me what an adventure it had been. Half way up the tower, his partner froze, and he had to help him back down to the ground. He said when he got to the railing around the tower, he looked down and almost froze himself, but eventually, he was able to do the job by himself.

At a staff meeting one day, two or three of us showed up in shirt sleeves. The Dean said, "we do not usually hold these meetings 'en negligeé ".

One of the advantages of being classified as a staff member was that I was invited to formal events which allowed me to circulate with people who were used to being in black tie and formal gowns. The usefulness of this was evident twenty-five years later when I was a Director of Alcan U.K., where formal dinners were quite frequent.

One of our toughest teachers was a Trinidadian who taught Zoology. Everyone knew that he would give you demerit points if there was grammar or other mistakes in the papers which you wrote. He set a standard which was an important part of our education,

When I did my post-graduate studies, I had Dr. Crampton as my lead professor. He was an American who really loved MacDonald and its campus. The first technical paper which I wrote for him, had some routine comments but when he gave it to me, he said "you have been spending too much time with Dr. Schurch", a Swiss post-doctoral member of the department. He was referring to the fact that my sentences were far too long.

Dr. Crampton also made the point that one is judged more by what we write than anything else that we do.

In the five years which I spent at MacDonald, we studied, amongst other subjects, Biology, Botany, Zoology, Genetics, Anatomy, Physiology, Pathology, Bio Physics, Bio Chemistry, Statistical Analysis and of course, during the post-graduate phase, the design of experiments.

A combination of laziness, football, hockey and inter-class water polo, almost resulted in my being sent home after the first semester, in second year. I had taken a Senior Matriculation at Westmount High School and went directly into the second year. This added two additional courses. About 15% of our class were sent home after the first semester. Some of them returned and did very well. One of them subsequently got a Doctorate for raising 15 million dollars for a MacDonald building project. He was a Managing Director, of a large sugar company by that time.

At year end, my exam schedule consisted of six in five days. I had to study very hard, particularly on Organic Chemistry, where you were marked on the cumulative marks for the two semesters. I had 30 out of 125, therefore, I had to make up the balance. Twenty-five points were for laboratory work.

When I wrote my final exam, I had 52 pages of notes which I could have re-written in total. This was when I realized that I had a photographic memory. I passed!

By Wednesday, my eyes were beginning to twitch, and I was completely exhausted. I lived in one of a number of rooms that had been created in the dining room which was

Owen, MacDonald College Graduation

built during the war for the Canadian Women's Army (CWAC), which used the MacDonald campus. The rooms had very high ceilings and were divided by eight-foot walls, each room had a closet with a ceiling built on to it.

Stu Horne only had to write four exams because of credits for studies in Britain. For some reason, Stu climbed up on top of the closet and started brushing dirt down into my room. I foolishly got up on a chair with the intention of catching the broom and pulling him down. He did not seem to agree, swung the hard-backed broom and opened a three-stitch cut over my eye. He took me to the Infirmary, we then went to the Registrar's Office to get permission for me to write my Thursday morning Calculus exam on the following Tuesday. One of the assistant professors of Mathematics lived in an apartment near the Annex. He gave me a five-hour tutorial which allowed me to pass the Calculus exam on the following Tuesday.

I never understood Calculus and as far as I know I never used it for the rest of my life.

In third and fourth year, we took an option "I think there were 12 ranging from Animal Science (which I studied),

Poultry, Horticulture, Agricultural Economics, Parasitology and Biochemistry - you get the idea".

In spite of the lessons of second year, I adopted my bad habits again in the third year. First semester I passed, but when I realized who had led the Option, my competitiveness kicked in because I could not accept being behind "that" nerd.

I led the Option, in third and fourth year. This was what lead Dr. Crampton to talk me into taking Post-graduate studies.

NOBODY PROMISED A BED OF ROSES

Shortly after we arrived in Arvida, our oldest son David was born. Followed later by Peter and Bruce. They were big babies, but otherwise were quite well. Richard was born several years later and was well raised by his older brothers. He is still proud of the day when he decided to find out what would happen if he stuck his foot in the spokes of the bicycle while riding on the handle bar. We think that he broke his nose but if he did it is still straight!

We had a wonderful life. A group of people from Europe created the Saguenay Yacht Club which was upstream from the big Shipshaw Power House. Saturdays and Sundays brought races almost every weekend. The participants had built their own Y-flyers. There was an excellent beach for the children to play. Later David and Peter took sailing lessons. I was never a good helmsman but the best sailor in the Club needed me on the jib to pull hard when needed and provide ballast.

George Balas was a skipper and an outstanding sailor. He later built his own aluminum boat and sailed around the world after retirement. His great pride was lapping other sailors before the end of the race.

I eventually purchased a Y-flyer in company with Al Buchli, the Swiss trained chef at the Manoir de Saguenay and Bob Hawrylshyn. Both of them left within a year and I had just enough understanding of how to sail that I sold the boat rather than be caught in a criminal activity during one of the races.

The boys were healthy. Bruce wasn't an athlete, but the other two boys were particularly keen on hockey.

When David was 12 years old, we took him to see the family doctor because he had been having frequent nose bleeds and was about to go to Cub Camp. Dr. Gilbert, our family doctor, checked the boys, said they were fine but as we were getting dressed to leave, he came out of his office and said to Arlie and I that he wanted to discuss something.

On visual examination of David's urine sample, he said that there was something that needed to be followed up.

We went to a specialist at the Royal Vic in Montreal who did a thorough exam, including a kidney biopsy.

When David recovered from the anesthesia, he turned to me and he said "Dad, why does everything happen to me?"

The doctors told us that he had the major symptoms of a genetic disease, called the Fanconi Lingyak Syndrome. However, he said, that some of the classic symptoms were not present and they did not know what to do.

Arlie's brother, Doug, was training to be an anesthesiologist at the Children's Hospital and he told us that we should see Dr. Scriver who was one of three geneticists in the world studying that disease, but it was more commonly called, Cystinosis, which is the incomplete metabolism of the amino acid. This leaves tiny particles of cystine in the blood system which eventually blocks the kidney. At a later stage of life, it causes blindness which now afflicts Peter. This is a double recessive genetic disease, in other words, the gene was carried by both parents. We then tested the three other boys and found that Peter was also affected.

This began a five-year period with a variety of treatments prescribed by Dr. Scriver and his assistant, Dr. Goldman. We would have tests done in Arvida and once or twice a year, we would go to the clinic at the Children's. During this time, the boys lived a normal life, particularly focusing on hockey in the winter, sailing and baseball in the summer.

The weather in April in Arvida was simply abominable. When we had the odd nice day, the cool breezes would blow in from James Bay and keep the temperature just below freezing. As a result of this, we would take the boys out of school to add extra days to Easter holidays and go to Florida.

In 1971, the boys both said "we played hockey all winter, there is nothing wrong with us. Why do we have to stop to see Dr. Scriver?"

Dr. Scriver said, "we absolutely have to see you".

When we went to the hospital, one of the technicians took the boys away to show them interesting things. Dr. Scriver, Dr. Goldman and two others in the research team took us into a small office and showed us a chart of diminishing function of both boys' kidneys.

We continued on our trip to Florida and stopped in Myrtle Beach for two days. On the second morning, the boys were out on the beach and as was our habit, Arlie was washing our dishes and I was trying to keep up drying them. She stopped put her hands on the sink and said, "if you're going to weep and cry like that, you will not be any help to me". That has always been my reminder of what a strong person she was particularly in view of what was going to happen.

We learned that both boys would go into kidney failure within a year. This turned our world upside down. In spite of Gaston Dufour's entreaties to please find a way to stay through the next contract negotiations, Arlie's brother prevailed and said "there is no way you can live 300 hundred miles away from Montreal, given what you are going to experience".

On the 16th of October 1971, David called me from John Abbott College and said I have a nosebleed which I cannot stop. His roommate had a car and drove him into Mount Royal where we lived. We got to the hospital around 4:00 in the morning. David told the resident that he was going into calcium deficiency. The resident disappeared for about 15 minutes (perhaps checking his books) and said that he was going to administer calcium gluconate immediately.

Later in the morning, Dr Goldman called to tell me that David needed blood transfusions. Heaven knows where I got the idea, but I said to him "aren't transfusions contra indicated before a transplant?". He said, "we will check and call you back". When he did, he said "if we use washed red blood cells, then it will not compromise transplants". He then added "we have made an appointment for tomorrow afternoon for Mrs. Ness, you and the boys to meet with Dr. Guttman, the head of the Transplant Unit at the Royal Victoria Hospital".

After the usual greetings, Dr. Guttman said "the ideal transplant is a parental transplant". All of a sudden, I am saying to myself "you knew that". For the next 10 or 15 minutes, I heard nothing because the only thought was "do we match the boys?" Months later, someone in the transplant group would mention something, and the boys would say "Dr. Guttman told you that, the day we met". The following Monday we discovered that I matched Peter and neither of us matched David. In mid-November, we went to the hospital for a three day work up to make sure that there were no problems to a successful transplant.

The surgeon who would be operating on me, came and sat at the end of my bed, the night before the operation, and started asking a whole series of questions about my sports activities, about other activities that would affect my circulation. I asked him if there was something wrong and he said "no, you have one of the best circulatory systems that I have ever seen, and I was only testing some of my theories".

On the 17th of November, one month after meeting Dr. Guttman, Peter and I went into the operating rooms. To show you how little I knew about what was going to happen to me, I said to one of the residents "when you've got me out, why don't you do a vasectomy at the same time". He said, " have you no idea what an operation this is?" I said "no, I trust you guys".

The actual removal of the kidney, which I am sure is much simpler nowadays, involves removing the small rib and an incision which goes around almost to the navel. The transplanted kidney to Peter was similar to an appendix operation. The replacement kidney is attached to an artery and connected to the bladder. He was out of bed in twenty-four hours.

The operation was on a Wednesday and I was kept "under" until Saturday. On the Saturday afternoon, a Brazilian resident came in to the room, and I was on my stomach, crying my eyes out. He said "Mr. Ness, it's all right, it's all right!!" I said, "I know".

I was in the hospital for over a week and decided that I could go to work when I got out. I put in a reasonably normal day except for everyone coming by to make sure that I was really still alive.

At 2:00 the next morning, David called from John Abbott and said, "they have a kidney for me". His roommate brought him in and I drove him to the hospital. While we were on the way, Arlie received a call saying that they had made a mistake and there was another person who had priority. When we got to the hospital, they told us that our luck had changed. The lady who had priority had an infection and they would proceed with David's transplant. There are always nail-biting times waiting to see if the transplant has been successful. It new kidney functioned very well but unfortunately, he lost it after 15 months.

Within a few months, despite admonitions from some of the surgeons, Peter and David had normal lives. They were playing in sports although not as much as in Arvida. Peter was a goaltender until he was over 45. Goal tenders who have their own set of pads are very popular on senior hockey teams. David enjoyed curling in Arvida and met his wife, Lucie, at the curling club.

In the early months, the kidneys quickly reached a satisfactory level of performance. Unfortunately, David's began to fail after fifteen months. When we took him to the hospital to confirm that it had failed, his reaction was "I knew it ", almost as though, he was pleased. This was one of the occasions when we learned that uncertainty or not knowing is worse than knowing even bad news.

We learned an even bigger lesson while David was in the hospital. A doctor from Saint John's, New Brunswick was in the same room as David. His three sons all matched and the oldest one insisted on being the donor. Unfortunately, the kidney failed after one week. As we were leaving, I spoke to the doctor and told him how much he had helped David during the three days that they were both in the same room. He said "you have it wrong! David is nineteen years old, I am fifty-seven, watching his acceptance of what had happened made me the real beneficiary of being together."

From 1971 until about three years later, all rooms in hospitals had four patients. These are some examples where patients and families helped each other.

On the day of the transplant, Peter developed a very high fever. The mother of another boy told us not to worry, that this was normal and a visit to the cobalt treatment the next day would bring it down to normal.

One of the examples of the four patient bedrooms was very painful for me. I had a Mr. Achanian, an Armenian, and Mr. Gomorato, an Italian, in the same room as I was after my operation. The nurse brought in a tray which was obviously to be used to do a liver biopsy. As far as we knew, it was for research on the side effects of anti-rejection drugs. The tray was set between the two beds and they started to tease each other as to who was going to get the needle. This was a few days after I had been stitched up. They made me laugh and it was the most painful laugh that I ever experienced.

At the time, Mr. Gomorato was sixty years old and normally because the process was so new, they only did it for people under fifty-five. Many years later, I saw his obituary, he died at the age of 80.

Later, the rooms were all changed to one or two patients to better control infection.

Sometime later, Dr. Guttman called me and asked me if my youngest sister, Evelyn, had spoken to me about the possibility of giving a kidney to David. David had already been on dialysis for some time. David, Arlie and I met with Dr. Guttman. David said, " I am absolutely not going to let my aunt go through what my father went through". Dr. Guttman very quietly took us through the reasons why that would be the wrong decision. He said "David, you know we do a lot of live transplants. As a matter of fact, it was over 70 last year. No one has ever regretted giving a kidney, even though as you know, some fail within a week. More importantly, you, Peter, your father and your aunt have a common set of chromosomes. Your odds of getting such a match from a cadaver transplant are very, very slim".

The transplant team, then did a very serious study of Evelyn's children's health and of course, a complete work-up for her. The transplant was a bit slow to function and when we went to see David, he said "look at the bag beside the bed, it's working!"

Peter got over 30 years and David 15 years from their transplants.

MORE ABOUT THE FAMILY

In an earlier conversation, I talked about the problems which David and Peter had in dealing with Cystinosis.

David earned a degree as a Chemical Engineer from McGill and to my surprise was offered a job with Alcan. The interviewers knew of his health problems. After interviews with several companies, David was most disappointed not to obtain a job with Proctor & Gamble. He asked me what he should have said when they asked about his health. I replied that if they were going to discriminate, there was not much he could do to avoid it. I added "if you could get some satisfaction out of it, you might ask them if they discriminated against people with medical problems". He worked in Arvida and in Montreal on a variety of projects. He enjoyed his work and particularly enjoyed being back in Arvida. He met a marvelous lady, Lucie St-Pierre, who came from the village of St.-Jean-Eudes near Arvida. They met at the curling club.

The kidney which he had received from his Aunt Evelyn worked well for about 15 years before it failed. He was then on dialysis for quite a period. He had a third transplant which failed in a matter of days.

One of the risks in organ transplants arises from the immunosuppressants which the recipients must take to avoid rejection. Melanoma is a very common skin cancer which is normally suppressed by the immune system. Around the time that David died, it was discovered that transplant recipients were quite vulnerable to Melanoma. The disease has four stages, where it starts as a skin lesion and then grows into the body. Once it passes the second stage, there is little chance to stop the disease, although surgery does slow it down. Melanoma was the battle which David did not win. He underwent a number of surgeries but eventually it metastasized into other organs. He was living in Montreal at that time and called me one Saturday afternoon, when Lucie was out, to tell me that the doctor had given him two to three months at the most.

In early January, Lucie's family arranged a trip to Arvida for David. He spent two wonderful days with a very loving family. About two weeks later, he suffered a stroke and when he got to the hospital, his speech was impaired, but he made it quite clear that he did not want any further surgery. He spent a number of days in Palliative Care and Lucie arranged to have two people with him, night and day, during that time. Family members came from Chicoutimi, Quebec City and the Montreal area. My turn came on a Saturday morning, when he was in some pain and I was not being successful getting them to give him some relief. When Lucie arrived, all hell broke loose and she said that she would go to the head of the institution if she had to, to get that nurse to do something to relieve his pain.

When David died, he and Lucie had already made all the funeral arrangements. He was cremated, and his ashes were buried in a small cemetery near the farm. Richard chose the location because he said it was home for him and he was sure that David would have wanted that.

In 1981, I phoned home from England on Easter Weekend. Bruce answered the phone. I asked questions about his exams and shortly into the conversation, he was having difficulty sorting out his words and then, he suddenly went quiet. I called David at the farm and told him that something was wrong with Bruce and to see if he could get help. At first, he said "Bruce was probably partying" but I quickly convinced him that he should take matters in his hands. He went to Montreal and by then, Bruce had recovered from his seizure, but he was immediately taken to the Neurological Hospital where they set up a series of tests to diagnose the nature of the seizure. A few weeks later, Bruce came to visit us in England. As I recall, spent a fair part of the summer with us. When he got home, he discovered that the hospital had been desperately trying to get in touch with him, because they had discovered a large brain tumour.

When they operated, they discovered that the tumor was putting considerable pressure on important parts of the brain which controls speech and other functions. They decided that the only recourse was x-ray treatment. The Chief Surgeon told us that with luck, he might live for another twenty years.

Bruce lived for eleven years, managed to complete his degree in Political Science and developed his computer skills. The seizures continued and made it difficult for him to take permanent employment. Bruce was a very kind-hearted person, always willing to help. He loved to drive and had an incredible sense of direction. I recall going to the Olympic Stadium and I said to him that he was on the wrong road, but he quickly proved that I was wrong. One day he drove us out to the farm and shortly afterwards had a severe seizure, and during the seizure kept trying to say something to us. I asked him the next day what he had been saying and he said I wanted to know if I would lose my driver's license because of the seizure.

After about ten years, Bruce received a letter from the Chief Surgeon at the Neurological Hospital, advising him that the original tumour had been completely cleared up. Unfortunately, some seizures were still occurring. In the Autumn of 1992, Bruce had some more serious seizures which led to him being hospitalized. He underwent some surgery. I met one of the Resident surgeons in the cafeteria and asked her if he had been diagnosed earlier would they have been able to correct his problem. She replied that these tumours were caused by the x-rays and were more diffuse. It was then clear that there was very little hope. He spent the next eight months with excellent care but after a few weeks was not able to function. In March, his principal nurse made it clear to me that we could choose to let him die naturally simply by reducing his food intake. I let my emotions get in the way and as a result, he passed away in July.

I think that Arlie and I realized that the only thing that we can control is to find the best possible care in this process of losing people. We were most fortunate to have had access to the best care in the world.

Peter had almost thirty years of normal function from his kidney transplant. He spent two summers as a fishing guide a thousand miles from Winnipeg. He later spent one year working in the Smelter in Kitimat. He was always a free spirit.

Front: Owen, Silvia, Arlie, Peter
Middle: Sarah Graham (niece), Richard, Lucie, David
Rear: Doug Graham, Bruce

He studied Law at the University of Ottawa, after the Registrar at McGill would not accept his credits from John Abbot College. He created a law practice in Stittsville with a partner, Ron Boivin, who was from Sudbury. Peter did the French business, while Ron dealt with the English clients. He later moved to Calgary where he went into business with a friend. Later, he joined a financial firm and worked there until he had to go onto dialysis because of kidney failure. Because of his age and rare blood type, we were worried that he would not find another donor.

Fortunately, he did get another transplant which was very successful. Unfortunately, the Cystinosis disease, over time, affects eye sight. It would appear that my kidney may have delayed that process, because Peter gradually lost his eye sight to the point of now being legally blind. This has deprived him of all the joy which he had, playing hockey as a goalie, curling, golf, softball and in latter years, training his dog to participate in a sport called Fly Ball. Through the Internet, he has developed a large network of friends. This is part of the positive attitude which he always displays.

Youngest son Richard celebrated his 50th birthday recently. Up until then, he had escaped all of the ailments which has affected the rest of us. It was too good to last. He was diagnosed during the same week with arthritis in his hip. It seems to be Osteoarthritis rather than the Rheumatoid Arthritis which has plagued me with a varying severity since I was 31 years old.

When Richard began school, in grade one, the school board happened to be approached by a young lady who had graduated from Queen's University in Psychology. Her husband had accepted employment at the College de Jonquiere. She offered her service to test students on a pro-bono basis if necessary. The Board accepted quite readily because a group of McGill students had tested grade 10 students in the previous year, showing the teaching staff how many problems could be solved with a better understanding of the student's psychological make-up. In his fourth week in school, his teacher recommended that Richard be tested because she couldn't quite understand what was wrong. The psychologist asked for a meeting with the teacher, Ruth Hutchins, Arlie and I. Richard had just turned six and his verbal abilities were equal to a ten-year-old (That's why we all thought he was smart). His hand/eye coordination was equal to a four-year-old and he had one of the usual Dyslectic symptoms of turning letters backwards and believing they were the same thing as the other way around. The psychologists told us that this gap, if untreated, creates tremendous frustration for the individual with behaviour which results from that frustration. She worked with Richard for the remainder of the year. I think a simple description would be to say that she was trying to teach him to see the world the way we do.

After Richard graduated from university and went into "finance", he had to write a number of exams to qualify for whatever they do. He was living with us when the final exam was to be written. I said to him "I haven't seen any sign of you studying for this exam. Are you not afraid of failing?" He drew himself up into his full six-foot three height, looked down at me and said "Dad, I have never failed in my life and I am not going to start now!"

Richard, Bruce, David & Peter

ARLIE

In January 1951, I went to a class dance which was held in the men's gym at MacDonald College. I was never much of a dancer but somehow or other found myself in a Virginia Reel which involves the couples dancing down between rows of the other dancers. That is when I met Arlie, dancing down the row showing all her energy. She reminded me of an older person that I knew. I then made it my business to know her better. We went to the Sophomore Prom together and later went to the Ice Capades with Jack Candlish and Beth Gardner. We continued to go together until the end of the year. I went back to the farm for the summer. Because Bobbie was away to Scotland to bring back a shipload of cattle and didn't come back because the ship was in dry dock for a number of weeks, then he was in quarantine for forty days. The result was that I did the milking morning and night for four and a half months. With farm work and playing on the softball team, I didn't go dancing. Arlie and I exchanged letters. She was working at Jasper for the summer.

When we got back to MacDonald College, the first or second time we went out, she told me that she had decided "to play the field" - probably not in those words. It took her a few weeks to play the field, then we became partners for the rest of her days. In the first year after graduation, she did her Internship at the Montreal General Hospital, which was located on Saint Lawrence Boulevard. I was doing Post-Graduate work at MacDonald. I would take the bus to Drummond Street and walk to the hospital. The street was called Dorchester Street in those days and was a favourite haunt of the panhandlers.

Later, she was at the Western General which allowed us to go to watch Junior Hockey double headers in the days of Boom Boom Geoffrion, Scotty Bowman and many other stars who later played in the NHL. We were sitting behind the goal the night that Jean-guy Talbot broke Scottie Bowman's skull with a two-handed slash on his head. Scottie never played again but became one of the best coaches in the NHL. Jean-Guy Talbot actually played for him later on.

On other nights, we would go to the Forum to watch the wrestling matches. Watching the women around the ring was the real amusement.

One night while walking down the street, I decided it was time to find out if she would marry me. To my surprise, she had already decided.

We were married in September 1953 in the United Church in the Town of Mount Royal with the reception in the Graham home. I borrowed dad's 1952 Chev and went on our honeymoon. Our first night was at the St. Maurice Hotel in Three Rivers. The next night we stayed at the Little White House, Bed & Breakfast, in Quebec City. The third night, after a full day of driving, we stayed at George Wright's home in Montague, Prince Edward Island. Our total amount of cash was $150, so we did a lot of "mooching". From PEI, we went to visit a good friend of Arlie's in New Brunswick. From there we went to see my great Aunt Alice in Maine. She had married George Bass whose family had created the Bass Shoe Company and were very wealthy. My first quality clothes were hand downs from the Bass family.

MR. AND MRS. OWEN MacGREGOR NESS, their marriage having been solemnized on Saturday afternoon in the Mount Royal United Church, Town of Mount Royal. Formerly Miss Carolyn Mary Graham, the bride is the daughter of Mr. and Mrs. G. P. Graham, of the Town of Mount Royal. The bridegroom is the son of Mr. and Mrs. J. E. Ness, of Howick, Que.

Ness-Graham Nuptials In Town of Mount Royal

We then made our way back to a motel in Bangor and from there back home.

For the next nine months, we lived in a hut which was one of a collection left over from the Residences built for the CWAC's during the war. Fortunately, some of our furniture was given to us as wedding gifts. We had one bathroom shared with the people in the other end of the hut. Locking the door was a very ingenious device. There was a stick that you put up to hold the other door closed. This meant that nobody could get in and you could not get out until you put it down.

I continued my studies and Arlie worked as a Dietician at the Veteran's Hospital. When I realize now how far she walked, four times a day to go to work at 7:00 in the morning, come home for a break in the afternoon, and go back to work from 4:00 to 7:00, I really appreciate what she had done. I wish I had told her then, but I can be a slow thinker at times.

Mainly as a result of my laziness, I did not receive my Masters Degree but it was already clear that I was not going to take a Doctor's Degree. As usual, I didn't have an idea what I was going to do but expected something would turn up. We actually looked at a farm. Dr. Crampton, who was a consultant for Alcan, told me that there probably would be an opening in Alcan for which I would be well suited. Many years later, I realized that Dr. Crampton had convinced Alcan that they needed somebody with an Agricultural background to handle their pollution problem. I have often wondered what would have happened if we had ended up on a farm. I don't think I would have been very good at it.

All the four boys were born in Arvida. The first three in a building built during the war, right beside the plant, in the area of maximum pollution. In September 1954, my grandmother died. Arlie was expecting the next week, I drove down to the funeral. I helped with the chores in the morning and when I went into the house, my mother told me that Arlie was in labour in the hospital. I made a quick visit to my grandfather, then made the 10-hour drive back to Arvida. David was born shortly after I arrived.

Peter was born a year later and Bruce, two and a half years later. Richard was born seven years later. We played golf the day before his birth.

We lived in a town house which were called block houses in those days. There were six houses in six different blocks with an open grass area between them. Two thirds of the tenants had arrived in Arvida at about the same time as we had. The mothers met in the morning around the sandboxes. When we went out to play cards or badminton in the evening, four or five children would be taken to one of the homes and taken care of by a local babysitter.

Our next door neighbour, Shirley Lindsay wrote Arlie's eulogy which is an excellent description of one of our closest relationships in Arvida.

I have often admitted that I had to learn to play bridge and golf while courting Arlie. She was an excellent bridge player. I often thought it was intuitive because she didn't bother with the complicated bidding systems which some people used.

My first attempt at golf was in a game with her mother, Mrs. Graham told me not to use a baseball swing, but I managed to make it through the game. Arlie played golf with another girl, called Janet McWha, who became the Provincial Champion. I still have our three trophies and six hole-in-one balls mounted as small trophies.

I used to feel sorry for the men whose wives did not play golf because in our last 18 years, we were able to play golf year-round. Ladies seem to enjoy playing with her and she made many friends for us.

Owen and Arlie celebrating their 40th Anniversary

We started going to Florida in 1963 when both her parents and my parents were in Florida. We drove her parent's car down and my parent's car back. We stayed in a motel type of resort, but the units were all separately owned. My bank manager talked me out of buying one of them because he thought that the exchange would become a real problem. It would have been a good investment. As I mentioned earlier, we got into the habit of going South until Easter every year. When Air Canada were trying to build the business using DC - 9's I paid full fare, Arlie paid two thirds fare and the boys paid one third fare. It was actually cheaper than driving.

Arlie was always an athlete. She participated in track & field in high school, and at college. Played basketball despite her height. Played ice hockey, at a time when ladies only had figure skates and later we both played badminton. We played as partners and discovered that playing in very competitive games, either made you quit or you learned how to get along. We achieved the latter. She was very, very quick at the net and I was able to hit the bird hard enough to play the back.

FIVE YEARS IN BRITAIN

In early 1979, David Morton was appointed Managing Director of Alcan U.K. In mid-year, he contacted Head Office and asked for my services. He had been in an office near mine during the time that I was Personnel Manager for Europe, Africa and Latin America. He also knew that the travel had me close to exhaustion. There were objections from Patrick Rich who was Vice-President for that region and he felt that his position was more important than the one in the U.K. He said that I would most likely inherit the position of Vice-President for Latin America. This did not appeal to me because it would have meant that Arlie would have to live in an apartment in Rio de Janeiro which to me was unthinkable. I agreed to take a demotion to move to the British job.

The three older boys were in university or had graduated, but Richard was going into grade 10 in high school. Dr. Thomas, who had been transferred from the U.K. to Canada expecting to return to the U.K. in two years, had brought part of his family to Canada. He told me not to do that if I could avoid it because he said that they had ended up with two sets of children. I decided to offer Richard a possibility of living on the farm with my brother Bobby and his wife Joan. He accepted and went to school at Chateauguay Regional with his cousin Linda who was two days older than he was. I thought that it all worked very smoothly, until many years later Richard said that I didn't know how much it hurt him to leave behind his friends in the Town of Mount Royal, "for the sake of my career". I should have realized that that had happened because of my experience with the many families that moved to different places for Alcan. It was always difficult for children between the ages of 12 and 16 when they were moved. I described it as birds who wanted to leave the nest but did not want the nest to move.

When we arrived in England, settling in had to be done quickly.

We found a good real estate agent and located a 275-year-old house, in a tiny hamlet, which belonged to people who were overseas in the Diplomatic Service. Such rentals were affordable because it was the period when people were in a house, they could claim squatter's rights and it was impossible to remove them. The only tenants that were safe were those who were on temporary assignment in Britain.

My offices were in Banbury, but the Executive offices were in London. One of the first times I saw David, he asked me if I had chosen my car, I said no, I am using one of the pool cars. He suggested I see the Purchasing

Officer and select a car. Terry Hayden, the Purchasing Officer, told me that as a Director of the company, I was eligible for a Jaguar, a Mercedes or a BMW. But I would have to wait 19 months to get a Mercedes. At that time, I did not know whether I would be in England that long. I asked the company chauffeurs what I should do. Should I be patriotic and take the Jaguar? They told me that it was a nice car to drive but a damn nuisance to get in and out of. That was how I ended up with a BMW. In spite of the fact that our company was suffering considerable losses.

My Industrial Relations Manager said that I had to have the BMW because employees would be annoyed if I went around in a car that did not indicate my stature. I later realized that this was the first time that the Personnel Manager was a Director of the company and he wanted everybody to know it.

This was one of the many things that I learned which were a result of the prolonged Labour Government. Personal income taxes in the 70% range had led to perks as being the way of rewarding people well down into the ranks, to the point where people being informed of a promotion would ask what kind of car they would have.

I had some interesting experiences with my BMW. My brother-in-law and sister came to visit us for a weekend and naturally, we took them for a drive to see the beautiful country side where we were living. As we left the village, in a slight moment of distraction, I was driving on the wrong side of the road. A car came over the hill ahead of us and some instinct or some would have said, the hand of God, made me switch to the proper side of the road as we were closing quickly on the other vehicle.

Shortly afterwards, I was in a pub in Banbury, when someone called from the other end of the bar and said "Owen, is that you?" I turned and said "yes, it's me" and one of my university classmates who owned a business in Banbury was visiting from Canada. We decided to go to another pub for dinner. Arlie had not yet come from Canada. As we set out in the BMW, I suddenly realized that I didn't know where the light switches were located. This was a manifestation of the fact that cars were never of interest to me.

When David Morton asked for my services, he realized that he had a huge problem with safety and he needed a senior leader for the group of professionals in the department. The safety record was abominable, we were paying large amounts of money in fines and the acceptance of such conditions could not continue.

David led the way by declaring "safety in this company is everyone's responsibility, starting with me". This brought the necessary focus, particularly in senior management, to make safety a high priority. In old plants, many bad habits had been developed and change was rather slow in the beginning. He told me that he was going to operate on a double entry system where Line Management would keep their records and report their results up the line. My responsibility would be to create the assessment line of reporting, essentially keeping track of the results. Stan Johnson was our Senior Safety Officer with long experience and did a good job for me. The following parts of my conversation describe some of the other members of my staff.

The early months brought a period of constant learning. I had a number of very excellent people on my staff. David Veall was responsible for training and development of staff. I was often the victim of his rather biting sense of humour. He was always straight forward and told one what he thought. One incident which I recall, was a meeting with David Morton to review our succession planning and the assessment of the prospects of some of the younger people. We started the meeting by asking David Morton to give us his "black" list. He was puzzled until we explained that he was quite dissatisfied with some of the employees and it was best to sort that out before we started a one by one review.

Except for a short period in Montreal, running the Corporate Planning activities and at CEI, David had spent his entire career in the Alcan U.K. organization. We knew that his judgment was more important than the information which we collected.

John Clark was responsible for Compensation. It could be quite complicated given the number of different companies which we operated. At times, we had difficulty understanding John. David Veall had a psychological assessment done and showed that John was a very brilliant person and at times had to tone down to the level of the people with whom he worked.

John was known for a short period as "Mrs. Clark's husband". His wife was an outstanding tennis player and was an umpire at one of the John MacEnroe's matches. They had quite an argument and people were impressed with how she held her own.

Len Walker who was proud of his Welsh roots was Industrial Relations Manager with many years of experience, particularly in the large Rogerstones Works. I had arrived in England about six months after the election of Margaret Thatcher. Industrial relations were embarking on a revolution at the time I arrived. There were occasions when Len and other Industrial Relation's people didn't seem to believe that the changes were real. When we merged the two companies, British Aluminum and Alcan U.K., I went to visit some of the plants which we had acquired. Falkirk, in Scotland had about 850 employees in a Rolling Mill. Everyone expected a severe cutback in employment as we rationalized duplicate operations of those which we already owned. Sandra Tulloch, the Personnel Manager, asked me to meet the Senior Steward on the plant floor. I had learned in my first months in Arvida Works that the appearance of senior personnel people talking with the local union was a wise way to behave when facing large changes. The Senior Steward said "Mr. Ness, I know that there will be large changes here, but I only ask you one thing. When the decisions are made in London, would you please tell Ms. Tulloch so that she can speak to me. I do not want to receive the information from the Senior Union people in London". I agreed to do this. When I told Len Walker, he was horrified and said that I obviously did not understand the way things worked in Britain. I told him that the power had moved to the floor and we would be well advised to recognize that.

A few months later, I had a similar situation with the Personnel Manager in Kitts Green in Birmingham. They were negotiating a renewal of their contract. I asked him whether there were major issues. He said that there were three issues, but he felt that they could settle by conceding one of them. I asked if these were major issues in terms of effect on the bottom line. He replied that they were not. He called me about a week later and said that they had settled. I asked what concessions they had made. He said one of the three. I then asked with whom he had settled? He replied, "our district official". I said that he would probably have industrial action the next day. Again, I was told that I did not understand how things worked. Unfortunately, I was right. The district official no longer had the power to make deals without consulting the workers. The strike was quite short lived when discussions included the shop stewards.

I was only closely involved in a local negotiation shortly before I returned to Montreal.

The Lynemouth Smelter was negotiating their contract at a time when there was considerable pressure for large increases. My brother-in-law, Brian Sawyer, was Works Manager and it promised to be a tough negotiation. George Russell asked me where Len Walker was at the time. I admitted that he was in Yugoslavia on holiday which had been planned much earlier. George ordered me to go to Lynemouth. On the first morning, Brian called a meeting of all the senior staff and explained that we would not move from the 8% offer which was on the table. After the end of the meeting, I asked to meet him in his office with Bill Patterson, his Personnel Manager. I then told Brian that with the exception of Bill, no one around the table believed him when he said he would hold the line. He was obviously surprised, but Bill agreed with me and said that the task would be to convince everybody from his staff to the workers on the floor. It was difficult but with an intense campaign of meetings, everyone knew that a strike would be of no benefit. Restarting a smelter after any shutdown is a period in hell for the workers. A settlement was achieved the night before the strike was supposed to start.

The day after the meeting with Brian and Bill, one of the company directors who was visiting the plant, told Brian that there were orders from Geneva to settle at any cost. He phoned George Russell who said that he would tell Brian what the policy was, not one of the directors on visit. It turned out that George knew about the order from Geneva but chose to ignore it. We realized later why Geneva was concerned, because the $65 million-dollar profit for the European area that year was from Lynemouth's production.

Why were Brian Sawyer and I working in the same place for Alcan?

In the second year after we went to Arvida, my sister Evelyn, known by her friends as "Corky", decided to come to Arvida to teach in the local school. Brian who had come from England was a Metallurgist working in the plant. They married and lived in Arvida. Out of the many young professionals in Arvida at that time, we crossed paths more often than anyone else. We had jobs in Montreal at the same time on three different occasions, and he was named Works Manager in Lynemouth six months before I was transferred to England.

Because we had so many plants scattered around the U.K., we had chauffeurs because it allowed us to work while travelling. Peter Callow was usually my driver. He was an excellent driver. He had been a truck driver and broke his back in an accident and could not do any heavy work. Just to the East of Ascott, the hills rose quite high and we frequently ran into heavy fogs. One night, we literally could not see in front of the car, but he knew the road and eventually got us home. On one of my trips, I started to feel sea sick and realized that Peter wasn't driving. He was also a good person from whom I could learn more about the community. As I mentioned, elsewhere, we went to the races at Ascot the month before we left England. I gave him his gratuity for the time he had worked for me. He had an outstanding day at the races and made it into a real sum.

A few months ago, I was described on Linked-In as a Financial Advisor for senior people. Definitely an exaggeration but I have done most of my investing. My years in England as a Board member were the training ground to understand what influences the markets. We were losing money when I first arrived, our shares were listed in London and I learned of the complexities of reporting operations, accounting practices and the role of consultants in influencing the market.

British Alcan Management - 1984

At one time, we had forty underlying companies with all of the complexities of accounting, particularly since our accounts had to meet accounting requirements of the U.K., Canada and the U.S.

When Alcan U.K. merged with British Aluminium, it was decided to close our offices on Berkley Square and move to the British Aluminium Head Offices on the western edge of London. Most of the staff in Banbury were transferred. I decided to commute because we enjoyed the little hamlet where we lived. Arlie had made many friends in a friendly hamlet which would not have been possible where the new office was located. This meant a sixty-minute drive in the morning if I left ahead of the traffic from Birmingham and a longer time in the evening because of traffic around London. It was twenty-three miles on a two-lane highway between home and Oxford. The rest of the way was on A-40, a three-lane highway which allowed me to pick up the Herald Tribune in Oxford and check the baseball scores while driving down A-40.

In the twenty-three miles, there were four places where it was safe to pass other cars. Unfortunately, some British drivers thought that there were eight places. Monday morning usually had the highest toll of accidents.

Shortly after David Morton left the U.K. to assume the second highest management position in Head Office, it became obvious that British Aluminium (BACO) were on the verge of bankruptcy.

George Russell who had replaced David, took the initiative and spent considerable time meeting with his counterpart, John Ford, to assess whether a take-over would be practical.

George was on the Board of the British Independent Television Authority which brought many contacts with government officials.

George was "politically skilled" and made sure that all of the authorities who might block the deal were fully aware of the benefits for the U.K. He dealt with the U.K. Combines Commission which is the equivalent of Anti-Trust Bodies in North America. He had Ullie von Freyburg, our senior official in Germany, deal with the E.U. and with the help of Lord Peyton, arranged a meeting for David Culver with Mrs. Thatcher.

The case for a merger was obvious. In the U.K., there were two companies competing in a whole range of products, in France there was one. In Germany, there was one, and all four were competing in the same market.

BACO had lost considerable money with the smelter which was based on nuclear power at a cost reputed to have been five times as high as they expected.

Financial negotiations were led by Denys Simmons from the Geneva office.

When the negotiations were completed, I had a few weeks of very long hours. George had formed teams to examine the merging of the wide range of businesses which both companies held and made recommendations for what should be retained.

Under U.K. law, there had to be a one week cooling off period after the announcements of the changes before discussions could occur between the unions and the company. Then we had to coordinate meetings with a huge number of businesses and plants. I worked closely with Jim Ramsey, the BACO Personnel Manager. We were good friends as he had been in touch with me from the time I arrived in the U.K. We were able to provide George and John with information on all managers in the two management teams.

Arranging out-placement for those who still had a career ahead of them, required the selection of a company specializing in out-placement services. I did this by contacting the largest head hunter companies and had almost unanimous recommendations for Pauline Hyde Associates. George advised one of the senior people that he was being terminated because he had developed bad relations with the BACO people who would be coming under his command. After George spoke to the gentleman, Pauline's husband spent an hour with him, convincing him not to go out on his own in the market and promised that they would find a position that would pay more than he was currently earning within nine months. A number of years later, the individual was knighted and can now preface his name with "Sir".

In the process of bringing the two companies together, we dealt with it as a merger, in spite of the fact that it was a financial take over. The action which brought the most positive results was the process of combining the pension plans. BACO had a traditional four level pension plan - four levels from senior executives down to hourly paid workers. Alcan had a single plan which applied to all levels. In anticipation of legislation creating pension committees involving the members, Alcan had developed a consultation structure which we applied to the new employees. Leveling out the pensions meant that most of the lower level BACO employees received better pensions. They also had to vote to accept higher contributions. It was very well received and made Alcan "the good guys".

After one year of operations, we asked the employees to make recommendations on the changes which they would like to see in the plan. We had a French-Canadian Actuary on our U.K. staff and they asked if they could have him as their advisor. Réal Provost in addition to being very competent, also had the personality to manage the situation.

Changes in the industry meant that we were constantly reducing and reorganizing part of the business. Much of the equipment was out of date and choices had to be made as to what we should keep. We had companies producing everything from safety glass to magnesium rods for nuclear power plants. The two companies had very different approaches in their ways of doing business. Some of the BACO perks were pleasant, such as a box at Covent Gardens and a box at Ascot Race Track. Shortly before we returned to Canada, we got dressed up in a lovely gown for Arlie and top hat and tails for me. These traditional things disappeared after a few years of being a part of Alcan.

It was interesting arriving at a name for the company. We eventually chose British Alcan much to the chagrin of some of management who felt that the name should have Alcan in front rather than British.

After all the travelling which I had done as V.P. Personnel for what was called the Atlantic Region, comprising Europe, Africa and Latin America, our time in England was wonderful with trips confined almost exclusively to England and Scotland. We had wonderful neighbours in the little hamlet of Ascott, Arthur and Rita Cooper. He was a retired inventor who was still consulting mostly in Germany and spent his time on a beautiful garden and restoring old Volkswagons. He told wonderful tales of the things that he had done, including racing at Le Mans in the early 20's. He developed quite a good business producing beams and posts for coal mines. Unfortunately, striking metal on aluminum caused explosive sparks and he had to pay the costs of removing all the aluminum. This made him an expert on the market for scrap aluminum.

After we'd been in the village, in the old house for two years, the owners returned. We purchased a modern house on the side of the valley. It had a marvelous view of the surrounding rolling country. It was owned by Dr. Naylor, a retired 92-year old dentist; born in South Africa and a veteran of the first World War. Negotiations were interesting. As is the tradition, I acquired an estimate of the value from the local "surveyor". On that basis, I made an offer. Dr. Naylor said that he had been asking around and we had nothing more to talk about. We went home to Canada for Christmas and when we came back, he had left a message asking me to see him again. He said that he had taken further advice and if I would make one or two minor changes, he would be happy to sell to me. We were both happy when I left. His gin & tonics seemed to affect my walk down the hill to our house.

Dr. Len and Vickie Selby spent weekends in the hamlet. He had a practice on Harley Street in London. She had inherited money from the Courtalds Textile Company. My rheumatoid arthritis started while I was in England, as a result of a visit to a very noisy plant where the manager apologized for his bad cold and by the end of the weekend, I was very, very sick and that kicked off my permanent immune reaction as manifested by rheumatoid arthritis. One afternoon while visiting the Selby's, Len said that he had the universal solution and served me a gin & tonic. Len and Vickie were Jewish which was only significant to me when one of his clients was a Saudi Arabian princess who had a brain tumour. He arranged for her to have an operation at the Montreal Neurological Institute and he and Vickie attended her wedding later in Saudi Arabia.

Len and Vickie were proud of their adventure in the "big April snow storm". On the Friday night weather forecast, we were told that there was a system moving West across the North Sea and another one moving East across the Irish Sea. The forecaster said that there was a chance that the two would come together over Scotland, and England would see one of the worst storms ever. On Saturday after lunch, Arlie and I decided to play golf, although the clouds were beginning to build up. When we got to the fourth hole, we couldn't see across the fairway. During the following 24-hours, we had 17 inches of wet snow. The Selby's set out to return to London and ended up staying with farmers about two miles from Ascott. English weather could be surprising. We had another big snowfall during the time we had gone home for Christmas. We made it to the village because I knew the main highways were open and the East/West stretch for the last 10 miles was clear because of the direction of the wind. On that occasion, the only food available for the pigeons were the brussel sprouts which protruded from the snow.

George and Mary Blencoe were our neighbours at the first house. Mary Blencoe was a lovely person. She had married George in Liverpool during the war and apparently did not realize the cultural difference. They had seventy acres of land on which he raised pigs, sheep and poultry. George was an interesting character, known to some people in the village as "Steptoe". Steptoe was the British predecessor to Samson & Son on American television.

The first Christmas, we decided to come home, and I asked George to check the furnace and make sure it was operating. Little did I know that he had never seen a furnace in his life. I did not really expect anything would happen, but my ignorance was quite extensive. I did not know that the oil could freeze between the reservoir which was outside and the furnace, inside. There was a severe period of cold weather and George did as he was told when he saw the red light, to press it and the furnace started, everything was all right. What I did not realize was that sufficient oil would melt near and in the house to run the furnace for a few moments. Most homes had cisterns in the attic. Ours was quite new with nice copper tubing leading down into the house. Of course, without any heat, these pipes froze and burst causing a major flood when the warmer weather came. The neighbour said it took seven men to throw the king size mattress out of the bedroom. They had already repaired the piping and the house was reasonably comfortable when I returned early. Unfortunately, the walls of the house were built of soft Cotswold stone which absorbed considerable amounts of water and when Arlie arrived, we had to cope with green mold on the stones which were wet. I guess it was reasonable that she should sit down and cry.

Colonel and Mrs. Bourne, our next door neighbours in our new house, was a veteran of the Second World War and his wife said that she had had 42 kitchens because of all the moves they made in the army. In retirement, he worked for the Oxford University Press and could do the London Times crossword in half an hour. They raised Yorkie Terriers and had a flock of geese.

Our closest friends were Derrick and Janet Haines. She obtained a membership for Arlie in the local golf club. On Friday nights, we would go there to play Military Whist. My most memorable hand was on a Friday night during the intense work period surrounding the merger of the companies. I was aware that I had made the bid but chose that moment to have a mini blackout. I could not remember the bid or the bidding. My lady partner was not pleased.

We would play bridge with Derrick and Janet from time to time. During lambing season, we would take a break at about 10:30 while Derrick went out to the sheep barn to check on the ewes. After a nice lunch, we would play until 2:00 in the morning. After we returned to Canada, Janet opened a Bed & Breakfast which we used as a base for visits that we made to Britain in later years.

As I often do, I was talking about nothing of importance and I recounted a physical check-up which I had had when joining a wellness course. I said that I had discovered that while sitting on the floor, I could touch the end of my toes with my wrists. When I first told Arlie this, she said "don't you know you've got short legs". Derrick and his wonderful English accent said "I've always wondered what else I could do while I was tying my boots in the morning".

A hamlet is a small agglomeration of houses which does not have a post office or a church. We lived in Ascott at the bottom of a small valley, a few miles off the main highway between Oxford and Stratford. The hill to the East was a dividing point where the water ran West on the one side and to the North Sea on the other side. A collective term for the villages to the West was "The Cotswalds". It was mostly rich farm land, owned by wealthy land lords and operated by tenants such as our neighbour, Derrick Haines.

While we were living there, there were still hunts on the Saturdays. Because of the rolling land, one could watch the whole proceedings from a high point. Colonel Bourne and his wife managed to divert the fox into one of their out-buildings causing great consternation. I assume that this was possible because of the number of dogs which they had on the property. It is almost thirty years since we left England, and many things have changed, including the hunts.

Banbury had seven pubs when I worked there. I think there are two now. They have been replaced by American fast food outlets. Our favorite pub was called "The Gate Hangs High". It stood alone on a country road which was on the way to Banbury from our house. Its charm was the people who came in quite often on a walk on the paths which wove their way through all of the farms in that area. The battle to maintain the paths was almost as fierce as the battle to eliminate hunting. A short distance to the East of Ascott, there was a road which had a ford. During the summer, it was easy to cross but there were occasions when the water rose quite high.

Because of the strict land use planning in England, it was virtually impossible to build a house in the country side. As a result of a loop hole, almost every unused farm building was converted into a house. At the rear of the Blencoe's farm, there was a building which they converted into quite a nice house. But an interesting situation arose, when the telephone company had to install about 50 poles to serve that house. It was just at the time before cell phones came in, but they had no choice and had to do it.

The largest nearby town was Chipping Norton. It was most memorable to us for the "Fish & Chips" shop; the chips were still sold in the traditional newspaper.

With help from the Works Manager in Banbury, I had a membership at the Tadmarton Golf Course. I played with a local doctor one Sunday and during the week received a letter for slow play. Most games are matches where the ball is picked up immediately when the winner is known. We were playing an ordinary game, where everyone plays out the hole and that was just not on when playing on Sunday.

The Alcan Chief Accountant, Colin Scarrett, lived in the next village and had a real English sense of humour. He recounted the story of an accountant at the Wembley Packaging Plant which was acquired from a private owner. This gentleman said that he had a problem as to how to make an entry for one of the salesman's expense account when he provided a lady to the client after lunch. Colin told him that it was quite simple. The entry would be "teas and tart".

When we were not otherwise busy, we would go to the local Anglican church in the next village. It was a chance to meet neighbours and was usually followed by beverages at one of our homes. I don't think it was our Vicar who originated the plea when announcing the offering "it is now time for a silent offering".

When we first arrived in Ascott, we were told that if we needed anything, the best place to go was to the local Post Mistress who would have all the answers about telephones, milk delivery, etc.. The lady was born in Cornwall, Ontario which was Arlie's birthplace. She had married the English manager of the Courtald's Plant in Cornwall. He was later transferred to England.

In 1984, it was clear that my services were no longer needed by British Alcan, because Jim Ramsey had all the qualifications, as well as an understanding of the history of the company. This was obvious to me, but it was not clear where I could go. I had even reached the point of asking our financial planner to work out what my situation would be if I had to leave the company.

Peter McGeer, Manager of the Kingston Laboratory, and Jeff Eddington, Manager of the Banbury Lab, knew me well. They approached their superior, Ihor Suchovrsky. They suggested that their boss, Hugh Wynne Edwards, needed someone who knew Alcan and its ways of doing things. I was offered the job of "Senior Administrative Officer" or something like that in Montreal, responsible for the Research Labs. In my earlier years, I worked closely with the Arvida Labs in my research work with the pollution problem. This made me quite comfortable to be back on "home ground".

A SHORT CAREER BACK IN RESEARCH

Before I arrived in Montreal, an announcement was put out under my name, appointing John Lajoie as my Controller. I had never met John, but he did most of the work in allowing us to make a substantial contribution to the Division. One of the problems was that the Chief Research Officer was new to Alcan and didn't understand the requests for authorization approval system. The result was that top scientists were spending far too much time with overly elaborate documents. John taught Accounting at McGill University at night and was the ideal person to teach anyone, who needed it, how to meet the financial requirements.

This was the time when Mr. Culver, chief executive officer, had declared that we were going to go into new products and by 1990, 25% of our revenue would be from those products. The nature of the products was unclear but generally had some relation to the aluminum business. The research people began research on a host of things of unknown future value. We decided to hire someone who could do early assessments of these projects. I am not sure how we originally found Mary Larsen. She had worked for the Boston Consulting Group and McKinsie Consultants and was looking for a job in Montreal. I realized at one point that I was bidding against the Royal Bank but having the knowledge of compensation plans which came from my many years in charge of compensation, I was able to build a package that met her needs.

Mary's husband was a professor of Bio-Chemistry who chose to leave Harvard to teach at the University of Montreal. Because the University of Montreal were very late coming into the Bio-Chemistry field, they had one of the most up to date research labs in North America. He and Mary were both from Montana. She had studied Ancient French at Columbia University and subsequently graduated from Stanford 'Cum Laude' in Business Administration.

One of the projects which she assessed was to produce a thin enough aluminum wire to replace the gold strands that were used in computers. She discovered that the total value of gold used (in 1986) was of the order of $8 Million dollars and it was highly unlikely that people would be interested in substituting the best conductor in the world with a lesser project.

After a visit to Kingston, she said that it was very discouraging to constantly prove that there was not a viable market for the products that were being studied.

She stayed in the job until a few months after my return to the Personnel field, where she helped me with some of my Personnel meetings. One in particular comes to mind. It was a meeting of all the Alcan North American Personnel Managers. At the insistence of someone in the group, we hired a Psychologist from the University of Montreal. People arrived at the hotel the night before. We had dinner and lively discussions in the bar afterwards. The professor called me at 5:30 the next morning and said that he was ill and would not be able to participate. The participants suspected that he had been frightened by the heat of the discussions the previous night. I called Mary and she joined us at the first meeting and was of tremendous help to achieve a productive meeting. Her degree from Stanford qualified her to deal with any business problem.

One of our fascinating projects was based on the idea that we should build the first all-aluminum car, this was Dr. Wynne Edwards dream of a major change for the company. All of us on staff had to sign secrecy agreements. Visits were made to Land Rover and a number of other car manufacturers. Fortunately, the attention was turned to working with the major car companies and the Kingston Labs made great contributions to hastening the use of aluminum in cars.

Alcan Top Management, 1989
David Morton (Chief Executive Officer) – front row center

In the early 70's, it was decided to reduce the Arvida Labs to a minimum operation to get away from the effects of Bill 101. Fortunately, much of this idea was abandoned because of the reaction of the community. I replaced Mr.

Ladd at a regular Tuesday morning Management meeting. Mr. Culver could not understand why there was such an uproar in the Saguenay when CIL had moved 700 jobs without any political reaction. I told him that there were four Federal ridings affected, directly or indirectly, by the change of Labs; whereas, in Montreal, the employees were scattered over many ridings. Nonetheless, many activities, which were not directly involved with aluminum were moved to Kingston. This turned out to be a good thing for many of their researchers who had joined the company in the early 50's and would remain in Kingston until retirement.

I visited the Arvida Labs with Dr. Wynne Edwards in 1985. We listened to presentations on the wide variety of research which was being done. Dr. Wynne Edwards said that he could understand what the goals were but much of the techniques were beyond his understanding. At that time there were six or seven research people who held Doctorates. They were all from the province of Quebec and had studied outside Canada. They wanted to work in Quebec and at that time, only had a choice between Alcan, Hydro Quebec and teaching in universities.

When Mr. Don McMillan was transferred out of the Arvida Labs, I had to lead the search for successor. I spent quite some time speaking to Steve Monahan who had spent most of his career in Technical Development in Arvida. We eventually hired the person he favoured most. The thing I remembered most from the discussion with Steve was his description of one man. He said "there is something wrong with the fellow because he smokes a lot and he's fat".

THE FINAL CHAPTER

In 1983 the public relations officer began his research to publish a history of Alcan. It resulted in three volumes and twenty-five hundred pages with the third volume being published in 1989. One of the paragraphs read as follows: "Owen M. Ness, a veteran of personnel management in Canada, the Americas and the U.K. was appointed to the top post, Vice President Personnel."

At that time Alcan had fifty thousand employees in nine countries. My job was to provide leadership to the personnel organizations in the various companies. The personnel department responsibilities included labour relations, pension plans and other benefits, worker safety, succession planning, the security activities and providing support to the various personnel officers in applying company policies. It also included advice to the chief executive officer.

This part of my career did not involve as much travelling as some of the other years. I organized meetings of about sixteen people who reported directly or indirectly to me. It allowed them to get to know each other since there was constant contacts between the various companies.

My chief security officer organized a meeting which took place in Kitimat.

The Kitimat security officer took the Irish officer out in the bay early one morning. The Irishman was scared out of his wits when a pod of killer whales came in from the Pacific. Security was of considerable concern in a number of countries. Perhaps Brazil was the most complex. In the early nineties many executives were kidnapped for ransom.

Owen Ness, Gerard DeSaintremy, David Morton, Doug Richie

I accompanied Jacques Bougie on his first trip to South America. When we arrived in Brazil we were met at the airport by four people rather than the usual one or two. When we arrived at the hotel the executive with us told me to walk up to the office with Mr. Bougie after we'd had a shower. When we came out of the hotel the extra two people fell in behind us and accompanied us to the office. I realized that they were security people. Later in the day when we were visiting a plant I asked Mr. Bougie which of them was carrying a gun. He seemed surprised so I said to him 'watch the lady dressed as a stewardess, it's in the large pocket on her jacket.

At a dinner with the board of Alcan, Brazil, I asked a senior banker if what we had done was similar to his security. He said 'not really, we always try to avoid being identified and take different routes and time to work and anywhere we go'.

It then occurred to me that Mr. Bougie had talked to the security man who reported to me and made these arrangements without my knowledge. It turned out that this was his style and when he took charge of operations he was often criticized for not sharing decisions with people who reported to him.

1n January 1993, I attended a seminar in Europe with my personnel officers from Britain and Germany. At this time Bruce was in the hospital and during the travel time I began to think about my career. I would normally retire in April of 1995.

Alcan had engaged a consulting company to examine the organization. It was obvious that major changes would be made around 1995 when the top personnel officer would be changed. He would not have been there during the studies unless I stepped aside. The more I thought about it the more it made sense to retire. Bruce was still in the hospital and that made me realize how valuable my time would be and my relevance would decrease at Alcan.

The board tried to get me to stay but it was eventually agreed that I would retire in July.

This was the period when tragedy struck. David's third transplanted kidney failed and he developed skin cancer. He suffered considerably. In the last months his wife Lucy was with him at all times. In January, 1991 Lucy took him to the Saguenay to be with her family once again for a real celebration of his life. He passed away five weeks later.

In 1982 Bruce developed brain cancer. Surgery removed part of the tumour but he had to have x-ray treatment which left him subject to seizures. He succeeded in completing his courses in political science and received his degree from McGill. In 1992 he developed new tumours and died in July of 1993.

Peter's kidney which had lasted thirty years from the transplantation failed. He was on dialysis for a number of years and was fortunate enough to receive a new kidney in 2008. Unfortunately he lost his eyesight and has been legally blind for quite some time. He had been in Calgary for a number of years and moved back to Montreal in 2008.

In 2010 Arlie and I returned from Florida for our medicals to renew our drivers licenses. She had been complaining of abdominal pains for some time. We decided to have a checkup. She went to Lakeshore General Hospital where she was diagnosed with a large inoperable tumour. After three weeks she went into palliative care. On her second last day she asked us to be quiet so that she could watch her soap opera.

A TRIBUTE TO ARLIE

The following pages/comments are my attempt to share the funeral service and a few select tributes to Arlie from her many friends.

Some People Make a Difference:

Some people make a difference just be being who they are. Their inner light shines and touches lives both near and far. And even when they're gone, they will forever play a part in the smiles, the priceless moments, that are treasured in the heart. In memory and celebration of someone who made this world a brighter and better place.

Text from the Funeral Service:

Arlie had a life with many joys and tragedies. Her response to these made her the special person we all know.

Arlie was born in Cornwall, ONT. Her father was an engineer at the paper mills. Arlie's mother died when she was 4 years old, the first of many disruptions in her life.

She lived with her grandmother until she was 9 years old, then moved with her younger brother to Montreal to live with her father and stepmother. This became a decade of happiness with her younger brother Mac and she helped raise her two stepbrother, Ken and Doug.

As Arlie moved through high school, she showed a lifetime passion for sports. At Macdonald College, she participated in track and field, basketball, badminton and hockey.

Macdonald was where she met Owen and began a partnership of 58 years. They married in 1953 and had 4 sons. Over the years, Owen's career took them to Arvida, Geneva, Switzerland, England and Montreal. During a year in Geneva, Switzerland, Arlie showed her true strengths: learning the language; learning to cook local dishes because funds were very limited while Owen studied international business management at CEI International Business School. She also earned her first driving license. This included the ability to back down alpine roads.

The 1960's were good times and included the arrival of 4th son Richard. In the 70's and 80's, bad news seemed to come at a regular pace. David and Peter's kidney transplants and then Bruce's tumour.

In later years, she was able to play golf virtually every day. It could be said that golf and her family, the grandchildren and nieces and nephews were her dominant passions. In

1971, before the boys had their first transplants, a move to Montreal had to be made. In 1972, the farm at Rockburn became the family retreat. The farm attracted family and friends, young and old every weekend, 10 or 12 was not unusual at the dining table. Arlie had to cope with this because she was the only cook in the family.

THE TWO MISSING CHAPTERS

In 1992 I was asked to join the board of the Queen Elizabeth Hospital. They wanted someone from South-Western Quebec because many patients were referred to the Queen Elizabeth. I did not expect that it would be an important role.

The hospital was undergoing changes in management because the director had retired after two decades as the manager. I was one of four board members given the task of finding a replacement. A headhunter had selected four candidates. Our chairman strongly supported an experienced man from another hospital. The nurse on the committee said that she much preferred Mario Lariviere. Because we were undergoing a lot of change I asked each candidate what he did with unsatisfactory performers. One of the candidates said he didn't have the problem. Mario said that he set objectives for all of his people but in problem cases he did a review every month and usually the employee would suggest that perhaps he should leave the company. This convinced me that he had the kind of experience that we needed.

On May 9th, 1995, it was announced on the news that the provincial government was going to close five hospitals including the Queen Elizabeth. It turned out that Paul Martin of the federal government had decided that the way to cut hospital costs was to shut some of them down. It was later admitted that they had to shut down one english hospital because there were four obvious francophone hospitals.

McGill University gave a well known writer the task of telling the story after the hospital was closed. The book is called 'Who Killed the Queen'.

In 1999, Jean-Guy Paquin called me. We hadn't been in touch for many years after I left Arvida. He said 'Tu doit te demander pourquoi je t'appel'. He was calling me on behalf of the retiree clubs that had been formed in Arvida and the other plants in Quebec. They wanted to nominate me as the retiree member on the pension committee. The Quebec government had put in a law that all pensions like Alcan's should have a committee formed by the company with a representative from active employees and a representative for retirees. They had agreed that I should be their candidate. I expressed my surprise that they would choose me because I had always been on the other side of the fence. He said that was exactly why I would be a good representative.

When I retired I had one task that I had not completed. David Morton had said that when we had made major cutbacks in 1985, the early retirement benefits were much lower than people who were retiring in the nineties.

Because of past activities I knew the chairman of the board and made the case to him and as the result the higher level of pensions were granted to people who had left earlier. The pension fund was in substantial surplus because of action taken many years earlier when the company decided to invest money in the pension fund when metal prices were high. What they did not anticipate was the inflation in the late seventies which meant that they did not have to contribute for many years from about 1986 and were still not contributing in 2001.

There of course was much more work that could be described in these two chapters but it is time to close my conversations.

In 1994 we purchased a property in Florida. We had followed Bob and Marcelle Goodwin and Rollie and Mary Racher. We still have the house and I have gone down every year. The community was called Lake Fairways. It had an executive golf course which made us both happy because we could play year round.

After Arlie died I continued to go down. Being an old community many friends disappeared. In 2013 our grouping of forty homes had their annual Christmas party.

When I arrived the table for our grouping of ten houses was occupied and two other ladies joined me at a separate table. They were new to the community that year. I bought two strips of 50/50 tickets and gave one of them to the two ladies. Arlie always used to win, I never did. The barrel that they used to mix the tickets tended to simply flop them over rather than mix them up. Annette Mariotti won three of the seven tickets. We joked about her taking us out to lunch.

Bruce, Peter, Hazel (my step-mother), Owen, Silvia, Richard, Arlie, David and Lucie.

One of the last photos of my family.

I went home for Christmas and when I returned in January I reminded her that we had a date. The other lady had not returned from up North. We went to the Sandy Hook on the water on the way to Pine Island.

When Annette offered to split the bill I told her that I was paying the bill and that I intended to court her.

In December 2014 Annette moved in with me and we've been together since that time. Unfortunately we both have medical problems. We are restricted to six months each in our foreign country. She likes to visit her family including two great grandchildren.

Owen & Annette - 2014

I admit that I was attracted by her beauty but I've learned that she can repair anything in the house and has an eye for beautiful furniture. She was a real find.

I hope that you have found some laughs, probably some tears and learned things you did not know.

Thank you, I have enjoyed reminiscing.

Made in the USA
Columbia, SC
20 July 2019